Successful
Television Writing

Successful Television Writing

Lee Goldberg
William Rabkin

WILEY

John Wiley & Sons, Inc.

Published by John Wiley & Sons, Inc., Hoboken, New Jersey
Published simultaneously in Canada

Design and production by Navta Associates, Inc.

Martial Law Beat Sheet courtesy of CBS Broadcasting Inc.
"Depths of Deceit" copyright © 2003 by Universal Studios. Courtesy of Universal Studios Publishing Rights, a Division of Universal Studios Licensing, Inc. All rights reserved

For general information about our other products and services, please contact our Customer Care Department within the United States at (800) 762-2974, outside the United States at (317) 572-3993 or fax (317) 572-4002.

Wiley also publishes its books in a variety of electronic formats. Some content that appears in print may not be available in electronic books. For more information about Wiley products, visit our web site at www.wiley.com.

Library of Congress Cataloging-in-Publication Data:

Goldberg, Lee, date.
    Successful television writing / Lee Goldberg & William Rabkin.
        p. cm. — (Wiley books for writers)
    Includes bibliographical references and index.
    ISBN 0-471-43168-0 (pbk.)
      1. Television authorship. I. Rabkin, William, 1959– II. Title. III. Wiley books for writers series.

PN1992.7 .G625 2003
808.2'25—dc21
                                                  2002191054

Printed in the United States of America

10 9 8 7 6 5 4 3 2

To Bill Yates for opening the door,
and to Michael Gleason
and Ernie Wallengren,
who showed us what to do
once we got through . . .

Contents

Contents

Acknowledgments

This book wouldn't be in your hands if not for novelist extraordinaire Walter Wager, who first suggested we write it, then relentlessly encouraged us to hurry up and *do* it.

We can't name and thank every writer, producer and executive who helped us along the way with invaluable advice and support, but you know who you are, and we are very grateful.

Finally, this book wouldn't have been possible without the hard work of our agents, Gina Maccoby and Mitchel Stein, and the patience and understanding of our wives, Carrie Rabkin and Valerie Goldberg.

So You Want to Write for Television

Most kids grow up watching TV.

We grew up wanting to live it.

We may only have been sitting on the sofa staring at the screen, but in our hearts and heads we were breaking into a foreign embassy with Alexander Mundy in *It Takes a Thief*. Exploring strange new worlds and kicking some alien butt with Captain Kirk in *Star Trek*. Pulling mini-flamethrowers out of the hidden compartments in our shoes with secret agent James West in *The Wild Wild West*.

We were just kids, but even we knew we wouldn't end up being spies like Napoleon Solo on *The Man from U.N.C.L.E.*, super cyborg heroes like *The Six Million Dollar Man*, or even debonair thieves like *The Saint*.

But there was one TV character we knew we could be.

He never stopped an entire universe from plunging into inter-galactic war or saved the world from a race of robots. But he did spend his days surrounded by the funniest, cleverest people on the planet. He got to come up with the one idea that would save the day when everyone else was despairing. And every night he went home to the woman every man in America wanted to marry.

His name was Rob Petrie.

And he was a television writer.

As anyone who watches Nick at Nite knows, Rob Petrie, Dick Van Dyke's character on *The Dick Van Dyke Show*, was the head writer for a high-rated sketch comedy program called *The Alan Brady Show*. And what a job that was. He'd sit around his comfy office with the other two writers—who seemed to be his best friends—cracking jokes and swapping wisecracks all day long, breaking only for the obligatory visit of the wacky deli man bringing lunch. He'd act out stories, craft sketches, struggle for just the right line, and when he was stuck, there was Buddy or Sally to help him out. He didn't even have to type.

This was the job we wanted. That was the *life* we wanted.

Of course, the kids who grew up to work for the CIA because they watched *The Man from U.N.C.L.E* found out pretty quickly that their jobs rarely involve hanging by one toe over a pit of piranhas while fighting a pair of identical fashion-model-robot assassins. And as both our sisters will attest, years of lawyering have never once allowed them to point to a witness on the stand and intone, "You might have gotten away with framing my client, if only you hadn't polished your nails."

So does writing for television turn out to be like the television version?

Absolutely.

At its best, a job on a writing staff is exactly like a job on Alan Brady's writing staff. Except we have better lunches.

We spend day after day sitting in comfy offices, surrounded by smart, funny, talented writers, all throwing out ideas on how to make a story work, or veering off into long, seemingly pointless conversations about politics, spouses, dogs, stocks, sex, and anything else that might clear our brains of whatever's blocking the story process. (On one show, the entire staff would arrive at around ten in the morning, then spend the next two hours discussing where we should have lunch, which is even more astonishing when we remember there were only two places we ever ate.) We crack jokes, swap wisecracks, act out action scenes, and struggle to find the right way to make a story work.

And for this, we're paid an obscene amount of money.

It's essentially like this at every show on television. Some writing rooms are happier than others, depending generally on the attitude of the showrunner (we'll explain all about "showrunners" later) and the mix of personalities on the staff. But they're all *The Alan Brady Show*.

In more ways than we expected.

You see, there was a lot going on at *The Alan Brady Show* that just seemed part of the comedy on *The Dick Van Dyke Show*. But when it happens in real life, it's suddenly a lot less funny.

There's Mel Cooley, to start with. Remember Mel, the show's producer? He'd come in, say the script was unshootable for some reason, and Buddy would make a bald joke and chase him out. As kids, we laughed at the prissy, uncreative producer and cheered Buddy for belittling him. We just never quite noticed that after Mel left, the entire staff started over again—on a whole new script.

Or think about that great episode where Rob is putting in all-nighters for an entire week because the script isn't working, and he starts to see flying saucers. As kids, we laughed at the way Rob was haunted by what turned out to be a prototype toy saucer (and probably drove our parents crazy making the saucer's *oonie-oop* sound for days on end). We just missed what now looks like the most important part of the story: *Rob was putting in all-nighters for an entire week because the script wasn't working.*

How about mercurial star Alan Brady, who would adore a script at lunch, then throw it out before dinner? Or the weekly guest stars who refused to do the bit written specifically for them? Or the way the show would sometimes run long or short or over budget and the writing staff would have to scramble to fix it?

All that turns out to be true, too.

Writing for television can be the best job in the world. It can also be hard, miserable, demoralizing, unpleasant work. We're not going to claim that it's backbreaking, exactly—although one of our staffers did once break a toe by dropping her laptop on it—but we, and every other TV writer, can tell you about weeks of sixteen-hour days without even a Sunday off.

And that's if you're lucky enough to get a job. As has been chronicled over and over again, the entertainment industry is cold, heartless, and cruel. It's almost impossible to get into, and once you're in, it's a constant battle to keep from getting locked out again. We don't know any TV writers who haven't considered leaving the business at least once in their careers. Most of us, fortunately or unfortunately, can't think of anything else we want to do.

We're not trying to scare you off. We just want you to know what you're getting into.

That's essentially the purpose of this book. We're not going to teach you the basics of how to write a script; there are already plenty of books, courses, and seminars out there claiming to do just that. And for the same reason, we're not going to bother giving you formats, templates, and typing advice.

What we are going to do is give you the information you'll need to plot a career as a TV writer. We're going to teach you how to craft a story for a particular series, how to sell that story, and—the most important test for a TV writer who aspires to anything higher than hackdom—how to merge your own style and point of view, your own voice, with that of an existing series.

We also want to teach the kind of writing that is required of every TV writer, but is never taught in classes. We're going to assume you can handle characters and dialogue and action. But when a producer comes to you and says, "We love the script, but we have to pull two hundred thousand dollars out of the budget to shoot it," when a network executive calls and says, "We love everything about the script, especially the fact that it's about incest, but we're moving the show to Sunday at seven. Can you take out the incest, but maintain the integrity of the story?" or when your star calls the night before shooting and says, "I don't care if I said I loved the idea of my sidekick having amnesia at story stage—I'm the star, and if anyone is going to have amnesia on my show, it's me, or I'm not coming out of my trailer," what do you do? If you work in television, you have to know how to find a way to make the changes.

And, absurd as it might sound under the circumstances, you have to know how to keep the script *good*.

We're also going to teach you about the business of being a TV writer, because as your career grows, and you find yourself moving up from freelancer to story editor to supervising producer to showrunner, you'll find that a greater and greater percentage of your time and talent is devoted to things other than writing—financial management, personality management, time management, star management, manager management, politics, conspiracies, and the occasional gunfight. (Okay, that last one might be a small exaggeration—most people in the TV business prefer to use knives. . . .)

We're going to tell you what showrunners look for in a freelancer and in a staff member. We're going to talk about how writers get hired and why writers get fired.

In short, we're going to give you all the information no one gave us when we started out.

Which leaves only one question: Who the hell are we to tell you any of this stuff, anyway?

In a word, we're writers.

We started off many years ago as aspiring freelancers, and we did what just about every aspiring TV writer does: we wrote a spec TV episode (*spec* meaning "on speculation," meaning "no one asked for it, no one wants to see it, and no one is paying for it"). In our case, the spec script was for a show called *Spenser: For Hire*. Our agent—we were lucky enough to have one then—sent it to the studio, where, after several months, an executive read it, liked it, and passed it along to Bill Yates, the show's executive producer.

He put it on a pile.

It sat there for a year.

And then something happened that we're going to tell you over the next couple hundred pages *never* happens. There was some kind of disaster at *Spenser*—a script that was about to go into "prep" (another term you'll be hearing a lot of in this book—it means "pre-production," and if the script isn't ready then, it means lots of money wasted) "fell out" (which means it was complete crap and no one could figure out how to fix it), and they needed a script in a hurry. When Bill Yates happened to lift our spec script off the top of the pile, it seems unlikely he was expecting to find something that would save him from plotting and writing a new script overnight; more likely, he was trying to distract himself from the notion of jumping out the window. Whatever the reason, he read the script.

And liked it.

And bought it.

And shot it.

And we've been working ever since, moving up the ladder from freelancers to staff writers to story editors to producers to supervising producers to, finally, executive producers.

And, in one of those odd twists that we used to think only happened on television, our dream came full circle when we found ourselves running *Diagnosis Murder,* which starred Rob Petrie himself, Dick Van Dyke.

Over all these years, we've worked with hundreds of writers, producers, directors, stars, and executives. We've taken innumerable pitches, and we've given even more. We've written dozens of hours of TV and rewritten five times that. We've taken terrible scripts and rewritten them into great episodes, and occasionally we've taken an excellent script and turned it into an unsalvageable mess. In other words, we've done the job.

But what's driven us to write this book is our experience hiring and—although this is the worst thing we ever have to do—firing other writers. A major part of our job is finding writers, for freelance assignments or staff positions, who we believe can give us the scripts we need to keep our series going. These are the most important decisions we make, and they're almost always based on one script. Sometimes on one page of one script. At most, on a couple of scripts and a half-hour meeting. (And that's a lot more than some other showrunners will give.)

It can be incredibly frustrating because we see people who have talent, who have drive, who have so much of what they're going to need to make it in TV. But there's something in their writing or their personal presentation that suggests they don't understand what the job really entails. And as much as we'd like to nurture new talent, we can't take the risk, because there's a network that's given us something like $50 million to produce a year's worth of episodes on time, on budget, and on quality, and we can't afford to bet that on a writer we suspect can't handle it yet.

So instead of the hands-on tutoring we'd like to give, we're writing this book in hopes that when your agent sends us your spec script and we call you in for a meeting, you'll be ready for your first job as a television writer.

1

Basic Preparation

To write for a television series, you have to understand how the series' concept, the characters, and the storytelling structure all work together. That's only half the job, the part you can see on your TV screen.

The other half is the business behind the camera, the unglamorous stuff that shapes, and reshapes, what you write more than anything else. It's where reality collides with creativity.

A television series is a business. An episode is a product made every week in a specified number of days for a certain price and delivered at a guaranteed running time on an inflexible deadline. There is a customer, the television network, that expects the product it is paying for to satisfy its needs and desires.

To write for a series, you have to understand how the realities of production and the demands of the network dictate and influence the stories you are going to tell.

A television series is also an art that involves the creative contributions of writers, directors, actors, composers, production designers, and many, many others, which means you have to understand the necessity of creative collaboration with others in the telling of your story.

So, ready to give up and go into the furniture business yet?

Now let's talk about the big question on your mind, the one that probably motivated you to buy this book in the first place.

How do I break in?

It's not easy.

What's wrong? You thought we were going to give you a magic word or a shortcut to get you past all the misery, frustration, and hard work?

You might as well take this book back and demand your refund now, because there is no easy way in. Unless your dad is Aaron Spelling, of course.

But you know what? It's not easy opening a restaurant, becoming an aerospace engineer, or writing a novel, either.

Television is like any other business. The difference is that everyone knows, basically, how to write. And everyone has watched a bad TV show and thought, Hell, I could write better than that.

But we'll say it again: It's not easy.

That said, here's the good part about breaking into the business. You have to watch a lot of TV. This means you can now sit down and watch thirty hours of TV a week and honestly tell people you're working.

Of course, this also means you'll have to watch a little differently. You'll have to start paying attention to things you've never consciously noticed. In other words, put down the beer and pick up a notepad.

The first thing you'll have to start looking at is all those credits at the beginning and end of every show. Ask yourself: *Who are all those people? What do they do? Who is in charge?*

The **executive producer,** also known as the showrunner, is in charge of every single aspect of a TV show: the scripts, the set, the clothes, the actors, the budget, everything. He hires everybody and he fires everybody. He's the one who gets the late-night calls from the actors complaining about scenes, and the early-morning calls from the network asking him to cut $100,000 from the budget. He's the guy who gets all the credit when the show works, and all the blame when it fails. The job of all the writers on the show, as well as everybody from the set decorator to the composer, is to figure out what the executive producer is going to like and how best to articulate his vision of the program.

And then there are the *other* executive producers. Some shows have four or five executive producers. Sometimes even *more.*

Unless you are a TV insider and familiar with the names, picking out the guy who is actually running the show isn't easy.

So who are all those executive producers?

Sometimes executive producers are the actors, the managers, or the agents of the key creative talent (i.e., the stars or showrunners), executives at the production company, or former showrunners who, contractually, receive a credit on the series for its entire run whether they are still working on it or not.

Let's use *Diagnosis Murder* as an example. There were five executive producers. There were the two of us, who ran the show. There was Fred Silverman, who owned the production company. There was Dean Hargrove, who was the executive producer during the first season and negotiated the right to receive that credit on the show as long as it lasted. And then there was Dick Van Dyke, who was the star and won the executive producer credit a few seasons into the show as a deal sweetener. Although Dick was not the showrunner, as the star he had an awful lot of influence on the stories we told and how we told them, and the fact is, he would have regardless of whether his agent managed to snag that producer credit for him.

Supervising producers are the executive producer's second-in-commands and are usually in charge of the writing staff. Because the executive producer is responsible for so many aspects of a TV show, he can't possibly do everything. For example, while the executive producer is in the editing room, someone has to meet with the writers, plot the next stories, answer phone calls from the set, and so forth. That is usually the supervising producer's job. If the executive producer is Captain Kirk, then the supervising producer is Mr. Spock or Dr. McCoy.

Sometimes the duties of a supervising producer are morphed into the job of "co-executive producer." Basically, it's the same as being a supervising producer, only you're getting paid a lot more money and getting a fancier title with more status.

There are two different kinds of **producers.** Someone whose title is simply "producer" is usually a writer whose duties have expanded into doing some of the casting, being on the set to work with the actors or directors, or helping out in the editing room. A producer is basically mastering the skills necessary to become a supervising producer.

Then you have what is called a "line producer." Unlike a writing producer, line producers are usually given the on-screen credit "Produced By." The line producer is responsible for the physical production of the show: the cameras, the crew, the locations, the building of the sets, the actual *making* of the show. The writers dream up an episode, but the line producer has to figure out how to actually film it, on time and on budget.

To make things even more confusing, a show typically also has **co-producers** and **associate producers.** Co-producers are often writers with just a few less responsibilities than a producer. Associate producers are usually the ones in charge of postproduction: everything that happens *after* the show has been shot. The editing, music, sound effects, color correcting, credits, and all the technical requirements for broadcasting the film are the responsibility of the associate producer.

Story editors are essentially full-time writers on the show. Their job is to do nothing but write original scripts, rewrite freelance scripts, and contribute to the development of the other stories and scripts.

Staff writers are basically script machines. They don't rewrite anyone else's script, but work on their own scripts and help break stories with the rest of the staff.

Freelance writers. This is where you come in. Freelance writers are outside writers who go from series to series writing individual episodes on a freelance basis. This is how every writer breaks in; it is the first, crucial step toward getting on staff, rising through the ranks, and running your own television empire.

But before you can start freelancing, before you can have your bungalow on the Paramount lot, six series on the air, and three exes to support, you're going to have to start looking at the world differently.

Well, not the *whole* world, just the one that exists on your TV screen.

So now you've studied the credits and you're ready to relax into the show. Don't. You can't watch TV simply for entertainment anymore. You have to study how the stories are told, how the characters are developed, and how conflict is dramatized.

You'll also have to read scripts and probably take a screenwriting course or two.

We're going to assume you've already taken the courses and have a basic understanding of screenwriting. But just in case you haven't, where can you find real, produced TV scripts?

Thanks to the Internet, they are everywhere and they are free (much to the chagrin of the writers, who believe their intellectual property is being distributed without their permission or compensation). There are hundreds of web sites offering scripts for downloading, but be sure you are getting actual teleplays and not some fan's transcription of what he or she saw on the air.

Lots of scripts have been collected and published in books, like *The Sopranos* and some *Star Trek* episodes, but you have to make sure that they have been reproduced in actual teleplay format, not reworked to make them more interesting to look at on the page.

You can also find scripts for sale in the back pages of *Premiere* magazine, where you will see classifieds for businesses that sell scripts. You can also find scripts at most university film school libraries, and if you're in Los Angeles, there are screenplays you can thumb through at the Writers Guild of America library and at the National Academy of Television Arts and Sciences.

But you're going to have to do more than just watch TV and read a few scripts.

If you were going into the footwear business, you would want to know how shoes are made, how they are sold, how they are advertised—all the things that affect shoes. The same goes for TV.

You need to learn the *business* of television, so invest in a subscription to *Daily Variety*, the industry trade paper. The magazine will tell you who is doing what, what the studios are developing, what new shows networks are looking at and not looking at, what shows are coming to first-run syndication, and so on and so on.

Now, armed with all that knowledge, you are ready to get to work learning to become a TV writer.

The first thing you have to know is: *What is a TV series?* And the answer is not as simple as you might think.

Exercises

- It's time to learn the business of television and get a sense of who the players are. Start watching television, *really* watching television, and start making a list of who the producers and studios are for the shows you enjoy. Update the list as the names change (and they do, especially around midseason), as shows get canceled, and as the producers move on to other projects.
- Keep a chart of the network schedules, updating them as series are moved and canceled, and new shows are added.
- When the networks announce their lists of new series in development in January, add the names of those writers, producers, and studios to your list and keep an eye on which of these programs are actually picked up as series in May.

2

What Is a TV Series?

"In the criminal justice system, the people are represented by two separate yet equally important groups: the police who investigate crimes and the district attorneys who prosecute the offenders. These are their stories."

"Space: the final frontier. These are the voyages of the starship *Enterprise*. Its five-year mission: to seek out new life and new civilizations. To boldly go where no man has gone before."

Every TV drama series is the same.

Sounds crazy, we know. How can we even compare *The West Wing* to *Baywatch* or *The X-Files* to *Diagnosis Murder*, let alone claim that there's no difference between the brilliant dramas of what some call a new golden age of television and, say, *Mutant X?*

It's true, there are great differences among these shows. But they're differences of ambition, of execution, of style. In terms of structure, of design, of production (in terms of what you need to know to make a career as a TV writer), they are fundamentally more similar than different. Writing successfully for *The District* requires the same skills, the same levels of understanding, as writing successfully for *Alias*.

Every drama series, for example, has regular characters and continuing relationships. Every series also has a four-act structure. So to write for a series, you have to understand how the concept, the characters, the storytelling structure all work together.

And because, as we've said before (and will say again and again), every television series is a business, you also have to understand how the realities of production and the demands of the network shape the stories you are going to tell.

Every series is also a work of art that involves the creative contributions of writers, directors, actors, composers, production designers, and many, many others. To write for a series, you have to understand the necessity of creative collaboration with others in telling your story.

Characters, stories, budgets, schedules, collaboration—we're going to deal with all of these over the course of this book.

But here is the most important thing to know about writing for TV: At its core, every series has a central contradiction. *It has to be the same show every week, and yet at the same time, it has to be new, fresh, and different.*

That doesn't sound too hard, does it?

Which takes us back to the question at the top of this chapter: *What is a TV series?*

Hey, that's easy. A TV series is that show that's on Wednesdays at 9:00 P.M. on NBC.

That's a fine answer, if all you want from that show is to *watch* it every week. But if you want to *write* for it, you need a slightly deeper definition. What makes a series unique? How do you define what is right for a particular series and what is indisputably wrong?

Let's start with this: A television series is the continuing adventures of a character, or group of characters, setting out each week to achieve a predetermined goal: enforcing the law, exploring space, healing the sick, raising a family, fighting monsters, or governing a nation, to name a few. The pursuit of that goal, and the manner in which the characters do it, is the framework for telling stories.

There's another word for that framework: It's the *franchise* of the series.

That's right, just like a Kentucky Fried Chicken outlet or Jiffy Lube, it's a template for a product that can be endlessly duplicated.

Really inspires creativity, doesn't it?

The first time we heard the word *franchise* in this context, we were appalled. We were writing a freelance episode of a Truly Awful Show for one of the most successful showrunners in the business, and happened to mention how much we liked a current series from one of his fiercest rivals. "It'll never last," he said. "It's got no *franchise.*"

Being the young geniuses we were, with all of two produced hours of TV to our credit, we knew this superstar producer was completely out of touch with the new wave of TV dramas. Sure, we were standing in front of his stretch Rolls-Royce limo, outside his $15 million home with the bowling alley, English pub, and recording studio in the basement, all bought with proceeds from his innumerable long-running hit dramas, but we knew there was more to the art of TV writing than something as crass as a *franchise.*

The show we liked was off the air within two months.

The sad, unbelievable fact was that this incredibly successful producer did know more about what makes a TV show work than we did.

What he knew was this: *It has to be the same show every week.*

The show we liked was something called *Stingray,* and it was an attempt to put a fresh twist on the action-adventure series. What we enjoyed most about it was that you never knew what it was going to be from week to week; one episode would be a straightforward action story, next week it would veer into science fiction, then it would become a caper comedy, and sometimes it would veer into stories so surreal they defied any attempt at genre classification.

To a couple of apprentice TV writers who had seen every episode of every action show produced, it was a fresh, exciting idea.

To the average viewer, it was a mess. If you liked what you saw in week one and tuned in for week two hoping for more of the same, you were guaranteed disappointment. Or, worse, confusion. And very few people tune into a TV show to be baffled.

When we first heard the word *franchise* applied to a TV show, we assumed it meant a formula designed to stifle creativity. In fact, it's just the opposite.

A show's franchise is the set of rules that *allow* for creativity. Without those rules, there's only chaos.

This isn't just a fact of dramatic television. Almost all dramatic writing follows dictates set down by Aristotle thousands of years ago. (Don't worry, we're not going to plunge you into yet another discussion of *The Poetics*. But if you don't know what we're talking about and you don't actually feel like reading Aristotle himself, just about every screenwriting book devotes dozens of pages to the subject.) Musical composition, classical or popular, follows strict guidelines defining melody, harmony, and other elements. Throughout most of the last millennium, even paintings were designed to fit into certain genres. It's the rules that define the art form.

Yes, the franchise does limit the stories that a series can tell. But it's those limits that make the series.

Think about it. When you turn on *Buffy the Vampire Slayer*, say, there are certain elements that you naturally expect you're going to find there. Vampires, for instance—or some kind of evil supernatural threat, anyway. You also want the offbeat humor that comes from seeing those ancient supernatural villains confronted by a group of very contemporary American teens. (Okay, they're moving into their twenties now, but the dialogue has the same zing.) You want to see Buffy kick butt, Willow try to cast a spell, Xander crack jokes, and Giles give that disapproving *hmm*.

Imagine a *Buffy* where none of this was present. Instead, Buffy is going on a blind date. He's a nice enough guy, but Buffy's just broken up with her boyfriend, and she's not sure she's ready to commit again. And meanwhile, she's having trouble with a particular concept in one of her college classes. And she's having money troubles, trying to find a few hundred bucks to fix her car.

You might actually make it all the way through this episode, if only to find out what the hell is going on. But if you get to the end and there isn't some bizarre, supernatural twist—oh, Buffy's been hypnotized by some evil demon to forget she's the Slayer, or something like that—you sit there staring at the blank screen and muttering the one phrase that's going through your head:

That wasn't a Buffy.

It's not that there's anything intrinsically wrong with those story threads. For a series like *Dawson's Creek*, a drama about the lives of college students, they're just right. But it's not *Buffy*. And if there were two or three or four episodes in a row that veered this far off-franchise, you'd probably stop watching.

That makes TV pretty limiting for a writer, doesn't it? Really cuts down on the kinds of stories you can tell?

Not at all. Because all of those *Dawson's Creek* story threads could work in a *Buffy* episode. They just have to be made to work within the franchise.

Take the blind date story. No reason Buffy can't have one. But you have to find a way to use it that reflects her particular character or situation. Most people spend their first dates talking about themselves and their exes, looking for things they might have in common with each other. But Buffy is the Slayer, and she can hardly bring that up over a piña colada. How much of herself can she reveal and how much does she have to hide—and how does she feel about that? Her first real love was a centuries-old vampire cursed to turn into a ravening demon if he allowed himself to find happiness with her; how does this new guy compare with that? And what happens if Buffy is actually starting to get interested in this guy when Slayer duty calls? How does she juggle her personal desires with her sense of responsibility?

Okay, so it's still not the greatest *Buffy* story ever written. But it does fall into the franchise. It *is* a *Buffy*.

In order to create a story for a series, you have to understand what the franchise is. Some shows tell you their franchise right up front in a song (like *Green Acres*, *Gilligan's Island*, and *The Nanny*) or with narration (like *Law & Order* and *Star Trek*, the examples at the top of this chapter). Some put their franchise right in the title—*E.R.*, *Family Law*, *Emergency*, *CSI: Crime Scene Investigation*, *Walker, Texas Ranger*.

How do you go about figuring out the rules that define a series? First of all, you watch the show as much as possible. (Yes, we know this sounds incredibly obvious, but you'd be surprised at the number of writers who come in to pitch an established series who've never actually bothered to check out an episode.) It doesn't take more than three or four episodes to begin to feel what's right and wrong for a particular show.

Understanding the franchise is the first step toward writing a TV episode, and frankly, it's our favorite, because it inevitably requires watching a *lot* of television.

The next step is just as important, and it means that you can spend a few more weeks sitting in front of the TV and you won't be lying when you say to your disapproving spouse, parent, or room-mate:

"Leave me alone, can't you see I'm working?"

Exercises

- Watch an entire night of television, and after each show is over, answer the question "What is the series about?" in four lines or less. In other words, figure out what the franchise is (and don't use any *Law & Order*, *CSI*, or *Star Trek* series; that's cheating).
- Okay, now that you've figured out what the franchise is in each of the series you watched, identify the principal charac-ters and their relationships. Save these notes; they'll come in handy for future exercises (and may have to be revised as you learn more).

3

The Four-Act Structure

In case we haven't mentioned it yet, all TV dramas are exactly the same.

That's certainly true in the case of script structure. Every hour-long dramatic series has a four-act structure for telling stories. This is true whether you're talking about *NYPD Blue* or *Stargate SG-1*, *Judging Amy,* or *Baywatch.*

Most of you know the four-act structure almost instinctively, thanks to countless hours of watching TV. The reason you know it is because you've been conditioned by the predictable rhythm of climatic moments in the story, the interruption of commercial breaks at the end of each act.

The four-act structure goes something like this:

In **Act One,** we are introduced to the characters, the conflicts, and what is at stake.

In **Act Two,** the hero (or heroes) embarks on a course of action to resolve the conflict (i.e., solve the crime, find the lost gold, etc.), but new obstacles are thrown in his path. The end of Act Two should turn the story in a startlingly new and unexpected direction. And trust us, we'll be talking a lot more about the end of Act Two in the chapters ahead.

In **Act Three,** our hero reacts to the change in the situation and the new obstacles it presents, and embarks on a new course of action that leads him to believe the situation is under control, but by the end of the act, he finds out he's wrong. The situation is much worse, or a new, much more daunting obstacle has been put between him and his goal. All the stakes have been dramatically raised. They are all going to die. There is no hope.

In **Act Four,** our hero comes up with a solution, overcomes his obstacles, resolves his conflicts, and achieves his goal. The killer is caught, the diamond is returned, the world is saved.

Even *Law & Order*, with its unusual format of dividing the story in half between cops and prosecutors, follows the four-act structure. By the end of Act One you know who died, you may know who the suspects are, and you certainly know what obstacles the detectives are facing in trying to solve the crime. At the end of Act Two, the cops arrest someone you didn't expect and turn the story in a whole new direction. In Act Three, the heroes (who are now the prosecutors) have everything they need to convict the bad guy. They've got the confession. They've got the witnesses. There is no problem at all. But by the end of Act Three, the judge throws out the confession, the witnesses recant their testimony, or the DAs discover they have the wrong person in custody and the murderer is still at large. In Act Four, they solve the crime and, more often than not, win the case. But whether they win or not, they always solve the mystery.

Virtually every hour-long TV show follows the four-act format with little variation.

A **teaser** is exactly what it sounds like, a tease, something to hook you into the show and make sure you stick around to find out what happens next. For example, every episode of *Law & Order* begins with someone discovering a body, and then the cops show up and learn something unusual about the murder (for example, a couple of joggers found the body, and it looks like the victim may have been beaten to death with a large frozen fish).

A **tag** is a wrap-up, a final comment, or as Quinn Martin called it, an epilog. It's the scene that lets you know the world is at peace, that order has been restored, and that the heroes are ready to embark on more adventures. It was the inevitable Spock joke at the end of every *Star Trek* episode.

Star Trek and *Diagnosis Murder*, for example, have teasers and tags. *Law & Order* and *E.R.* have teasers but don't have tags. Some shows, particularly in first-run syndication, have teasers and tags and also divide two of their four acts in half to cram in more commercials. But despite these permutations, they all rigidly conform to the same basic structure. Every producer you pitch to will expect your story to follow that structure. Before you can begin a career in television, you must master that storytelling skill.

One way to do this is to record several episodes of different series, then sit down and analyze the stories. What were the act breaks? In other words, what were the key scenes before each commercial, and how did those scenes advance the story, raise the stakes for the characters, and create new conflict?

Once you understand the four-act structure, you're ready to move on to creating a story for a TV show.

But what makes a good TV story? And how do you tell it within the constraints of the four-act structure? And how do you do all that while staying true to the franchise of the series?

Scary, isn't it?

Actually, it's easier than you might think, because the story doesn't really matter anyway.

What!?

Let us explain . . .

Exercises

- Watch an episode of a show. Stop after each act. Describe in one sentence the narrative arc of each act. Also describe, in a line or two, what happens in the final scene of each act. You will end up with a clear diagram of the four-act structure and how it works narratively.
- Look at the Act Two break of several hour-long TV episodes. Analyze how the moment, scene, or revelation at the end of Act Two changes the direction of the story.

4

Telling a TV Story

Ask just about anyone in the TV business, and they'll tell you the same thing: No one watches their favorite shows for the stories.

People don't watch shows to see a closing argument in a courtroom, a car chase through downtown Los Angeles, or an interstellar battle. They watch to see what happens to the characters they love.

People tune into *Buffy the Vampire Slayer* to see how the supernatural is going to affect her life, not to see the monster of the week. People tune into *NYPD Blue* to see how Sipowicz solves a crime and how he deals with it. They really don't care what the crime is, or who did it. They care about how it affects Sipowicz.

Ask just about any TV writer, and he'll tell you the same thing: The worst part of the job is sitting in that damn room day after day, trying to make a story work.

Why do we bother? If nobody really cares about the story, why do we spend so much time on it?

We're going to answer that, but before we do, we'd better deal with the outraged reader—yeah, that's you in the striped shirt—who's about to toss this book across the room because of our ridiculous pronouncement that story doesn't matter in TV.

Let's try a simple exercise. Pick a series at random. Got one? Good, we've all chosen the same show—*Star Trek*, the original series. Think back over all the episodes you can remember quickly. What comes to mind?

The stories, you say. Kirk and Spock beam down to a planet of gangsters. A planet of Romans. A planet of Native Americans.

But those aren't stories. They're one-line ideas for stories—what we call **areas.** The actual story is what happens over the course of the entire episode. Can you remember what Kirk and Spock are supposed to be doing on the Roman planet? Why it's so important that they visit the Native American planet? How they bring peace and justice to the gangster world?

Of course not. (And if you can, you really ought to get out more.) What we remember from those episodes is moments: moments of suspense, moments of humor, and most of all, moments of character. Captain Kirk in the arena, fighting as a gladiator. Spock in a pin-striped suit, mangling Chicago gang slang. Kirk, his shirt torn, dramatically intoning the Declaration of Independence as if he's preparing to record it as a follow-up to "Lucy in the Sky with Diamonds."

This is what TV is all about.

So we go back to our question: Why do we bother killing ourselves to make that story work when all anybody is going to remember is that killer scene at the end of Act Three?

We do it because we know the story is the framework that makes the killer scene at the end of Act Three possible.

The audience may be tuning in to watch its favorite characters, but those characters can work only if they're placed in the right context, if they're given challenges, risks, perils, adversities.

Think back to the pilot of *The West Wing*, if you can. There's a brilliant moment in the fourth act when Josh and Toby are meeting with three representatives of the Christian right, one of whom Josh has insulted on national television. Somehow all five people get into a heated debate over the order of the Ten Commandments. What is the First Commandment? And that's when we hear the off-screen voice of President Josiah Bartlett, appearing for the first time in the episode (and, obviously, since this is the pilot, the series), intoning, "*I am the Lord thy God. Thou shalt have no other god before Me.*"

Even taken out of context, it's a great introduction to a bigger-than-life character, and if this had been a stand-alone scene, it would still have gotten a grin from us as viewers. But in the context of the story, it's a defining moment in the series. Much of the preceding three acts have been concerned with the question, Now that Josh has insulted the Christian right, how will the president deal with them? Will he be forced to fire Josh? Will he in addition have to make major policy concessions? Is this administration going to cave in to one of their most serious adversaries? When Bartlett comes in, not only quoting the Bible but knowing it better than the religious extremists who have wrapped themselves in it—and identifying himself with God and against them—it feels like Luke Skywalker blowing up the Death Star. It's a stand-up-and-cheer moment.

This scene will join all the others in our heads, TV moments that will swim into our minds unbidden over the years. But the reason it's there is not only the excellence of the scene itself, but the emotions it carries. And it carries those emotions only because of the context of the story.

And before you can create those scenes of great emotional impact, you have to figure out what kind of story will lead you to them.

Which brings us to a Thursday afternoon in midautumn about ten years ago, at just about three o'clock in the afternoon. Six writers, slightly groggy from a too-heavy Cuban lunch, sit silently, staring into space, avoiding each other's gaze. Six writers whose combined credits include everything from Emmy-winning family shows and serious medical dramas to superhero and detective shows and nighttime soaps, and not one of them says a word.

It's Thursday, three o'clock in the afternoon, and we're already halfway through our prep week on the next episode, and we don't have a script. Or a story. Not even a notion.

Finally the supervising producer stands up, throws his notepad in the trash, and shouts: "I could come up with stories for the Home Shopping Network and I can't think of a single idea for this damn show."

Why was it so hard? After all, coming up with stories is what we do.

Part of the problem was the series itself—it was *Baywatch*, now known as a worldwide phenomenon, but at the time a struggling first-year drama on NBC with a franchise that made it particularly difficult to craft stories. If, as we all tended to mutter at least five times every day, you're writing about a detective, or a cop, or a doctor, it's fairly easy: a client/victim/patient comes to your hero and says, "I have a problem," and the hero spends the next hour trying to solve it. With lifeguards, someone's drowning, so you dive into the water, pull her out, and send her on her way. Story's over—and you haven't even hit the opening credits yet.

Of course, that excuse would sound a lot less lame if *Baywatch* hadn't gone on to run for something like 650 million episodes, each one featuring at the very least one story.

Although we didn't realize it at the time, the problem we had on *Baywatch* was not that we couldn't come up with a story.

It was that we hadn't come up with THE story.

Every writer in that room knew what went into a good story. But not one of us had a clue what we needed for a good *Baywatch* story. We hadn't found our template yet.

Remember, for a TV show to have a successful season, it needs twenty-two stories that are all fresh, new, and different—*and at the same time are all exactly the same*.

The question we were facing on *Baywatch* is faced by every staff on a new show—*the same as what?* Which story elements are unique to one episode, and which ones will form the building blocks for the rest of the series?

We had already done eight or nine episodes, throwing stories up on the screen and trying to figure out which ones were going to define the series. Our executive producer, brought in to replace the creators after the pilot and therefore as lost as any of us, wrote the first episode, a loosely structured overview of our lifeguards' hard work during the hottest day of the year. It serviced to show what our heroes did, but there was no central conflict driving it—had that episode served as our template, the show would have turned into a lifeguard version of *Adam 12*. Maybe that wouldn't have been such a bad thing, but at the time, none of us could figure out how to make the series work that way.

Over the next weeks, we kept trying stories. Any stories. Two bickering small-time crooks crash their plane into the bay and spend the hour trying to scam the lifeguards into recovering their stolen loot, which is now underwater. (Made our heroes look like fools—and do we really want to turn our lifeguards into crime fighters?)

An old girlfriend of Mitch's (David Hasselhoff) returns for a class reunion and reveals that while they were dating, she was also sleeping with Mitch's best friend, Craig (Parker Stevenson). (What does this have to do with lifeguards? Or with the beach?)

Eddie (Billy Warlock) has to face his troubled past when an old rival from the mean streets of Detroit—or some other urban center with streets of equal meanness—comes to settle a score. (Again, what does this have to do with what people tuned into *Baywatch* to see—lifeguards?)

In the middle of a violent storm, three desperate criminals hide out in Baywatch headquarters and hold all the lifeguards hostage. (Bet you've never seen this one before. But on *Baywatch*, we could make this one uniquely our own because it was *lifeguards* who were held hostage. Right.)

A beautiful young girl runs away from her mobster boyfriend and hides out in lifeguard rookie school. (A bad idea rendered ludicrous by the lifeguard connection—the arguments among the staff over how to manipulate this girl into rookie school were much more entertaining than anything we put on film. And, oh yeah, all these scripts were weekend gang bangs—shows so far behind schedule the entire staff churned them out over the weekend before shooting— and guess which two writers got credit for "*Rookie School*"?)

Six, seven, eight episodes in, nothing was really working. There wasn't a single episode we could point to and say, "*That* is a *Baywatch*." But that long Thursday afternoon was our turning point. Because in a moment of despair, one staff member (okay, it was one of us) uttered the dumbest story idea anyone had ever heard:

Eddie and Shauni are trapped in the back of an armored car at the bottom of Santa Monica Bay.

How did they get in the armored car? Didn't know. How were they going to escape? No clue. What the hell is an armored car doing at the bottom of Santa Monica Bay? We'd figure something out.

27

Despite its improbability, despite its outright stupidity, there was something about this that sounded like it might be a *Baywatch*.

God knows, you couldn't do it on any other series.

While the executive producer ran out of the room to alert the department heads to the fact we'd be wanting to dump an armored car into the bay next week, the other writers stayed behind and beat the story out. We slammed out the script over the (long, long) weekend, and Monday morning we were on Santa Monica Pier to watch the truck go into the water.

This would be a perfect tale if we could end it by saying the episode turned out great. It didn't. In fact, *Rolling Stone* magazine, in an overview of the fall TV season, called it one of the worst hours of television ever. They were being kind.

But in a way, that episode saved our season, because it provided us with the template we needed for the show: Our main story would be a big physical disaster, and we would surround that with personal stories that revolved around that crisis. An earthquake. A dangerous gambling boat sinking in the Pacific. A deadly speedboat race. All of these could provide the tentpole needed to support our episodes, and spin off enough B and C stories to keep our large cast busy.

Sure, it sounds obvious now. It felt obvious the moment we hit on it. The right answer almost always does.

The rest of the season was a breeze. Now that we knew what the series was, we also knew instinctively what it *wasn't*. Our story sessions became much shorter, much happier, and much more productive. And with the stories flowing freely, we could focus more attention on our characters.

Don't misunderstand—we're not going to claim that the second half-season of *Baywatch* on NBC was brilliantly written. It wasn't. But we had learned how to tell stories for the series, and we could have kept coming up with them for years to come. (Fortunately, we were canceled, so we didn't have to.)

It sounds terribly formulaic, doesn't it? You come up with one story, and then you spend the rest of the season churning out Xeroxes of it every week? Doesn't that make you a *hack*?

Well, you know what Goethe says:

"In der Beschrankung zeigt sich der Meister."

Or, if your German is a little rusty:

"In the limitations the master shows his mastery."

Or, in TV-speak:

"It has to be the same show every week, and yet at the same time, it has to be new, fresh, and different."

You know that almost every episode of *The West Wing* will be fundamentally similar—not unlike our style of *Baywatch* stories, actually, but with some political crisis taking the place of our multiple-life-threatening disaster. But within that standard structure, that *formula*, the writers are able to explore the lives, intellects, and emotions of their characters.

Now that you've mastered the four-act structure and understand what makes a good TV story, it's time to tackle your most important task as an aspiring TV writer: writing the spec script.

Exercise

- Watch three episodes of a show and ask yourself what their stories have in common and why they couldn't be told on any other series. Isolate the elements that make these three episodes different from each other, and yet the same. (Yes, we know it sounds like a contradiction, but it really isn't, not in series television!)

5

The Spec Script

No one asked for it.

No one's paying for it.

No one wants to read it.

It's a pitiful thing, the episodic spec script.

Granted, lots of valuable writing has been done on spec. Almost every first novel. The vast majority of plays. Innumerable great movies. Just about the entire canon of English-language poetry.

But all of that work was done with an expectation—or at least a hope—that it would someday find an audience. Every writer who has walled himself up in a cork-lined attic or a dingy basement, putting his life on hold so he can ease (or force) his words onto paper, feels the sacrifice will finally be worth it when his work reaches publishers or producers. Then its genius will be hailed, its art extolled, its contribution to society recognized.

And oh, yeah, he'll finally start making some real money.

But an aspiring TV writer who sits down to write a spec episode doesn't have that hope. He's got to know that this script will never be produced, and at most will be read by a couple hundred people who'd rather be doing just about anything else.

And no one will ever pay him a nickel for all that work.

And once the spec has made its rounds of agencies and—if the writer is lucky enough to land an agent—production companies and executive producers, its useful life is over. A screenwriter or playwright, finding doors slammed in his face, can rent a digital video camera to film his own script or set up a stage in Dad's barn to produce his own play. But the best digital video in the world can't turn your spec episode into an actual *Law & Order*.

To put it bluntly, the odds are that writing a spec episodic script will turn out to be the biggest waste of time in your life—and that includes the forty-eight hours you spent on the couch watching TV Land's weekend-long *McHale's Navy* marathon.

So why do it?

Because it's the only way in.

You may know in your heart that you're the equal of Aaron Sorkin and David E. Kelley, but there are very few people who are going to take that on faith. Unless your mother is running a network, you're going to have to show some proof.

(Granted, there are some writers who never do write a spec episode. But they're generally writers who have proven themselves in another field. Many of them come from feature films—Sorkin was a playwright who became an Academy Award–nominated screenwriter; Kevin Williamson created a billion-dollar movie franchise with *Scream*; J. J. Abrams was one of the writers on *Armageddon*— but studios have also made writing deals with Pulitzer-winning cartoonists like Gary Trudeau and best-selling novelists like Caleb Carr, Stephen King, and Tom Clancy. If you fall into any of the above categories, you may skip ahead to the next chapter.)

That proof is going to have to take the form of an episodic script. Although there are some producers who prefer to read screenplays, most showrunners, agents, and network executives will have questions that can only be answered by a TV script. Even if your spec feature script has acceptable levels of dialogue, characterization, and structure, people thinking of hiring you will still wonder, Yes, but can he handle *my* characters? An original piece will—must— demonstrate that you have your own voice as a writer, but can you blend that voice with ours? Can you write what we need without losing whatever it is that makes you unique?

That's why we need to see your talents applied to a TV episode. To someone else's characters. To someone else's voice.

Also, let's be honest. A feature script will weigh in somewhere north of 100 pages; a TV spec is rarely more than 65. It's a given that when development execs—okay, and sometimes even other writers—are grabbing scripts to read from that giant, ever-growing pile, it's just like when you formed softball teams in elementary school: The fat ones are always the last to be picked.

One way people get around the despair of writing something as useless as a spec episode is to think of it as a calling card. But it's really much more than that—after all, what's a calling card but a piece of paper announcing that you're waiting? The spec is actually your advance guard, your ambassador. It can sneak past the gates of the studios and networks and, once in, convince the people within of your genius.

Assuming, of course, that your spec script is as good as you think it is.

Exercises

- Make five strong arguments explaining why you shouldn't have to write a spec script to get a job in TV.
- Tear those five arguments up and get to work.

6

What to Spec?

Whenever we speak to aspiring TV writers, we are always asked two questions:

"I've never written a script in my life, but I have a great idea for a series. How can I sell it?"

and

"I want to write a spec. What show should I use?"

We'll tackle the first question later in this book (hint: the answer never makes the questioner happy), but the second deserves some consideration here.

In the endless series of decisions that goes into writing any script (Should he say this or that? Will she live or die? Do I reveal this bit of information in Act One or Act Four?), there are few that will be as important as this one. So in the great tradition of sages and gurus throughout history, we're going to throw the answer back to you:

I dunno. What show do you like?

Yeah, it really is that simple.

Almost.

But we'll get to that *almost* in a minute. Let's deal with the simple part first.

What show do you like?

It's a serious decision to spec a particular series; it means devoting a good chunk of the next few weeks or months to a particular set of characters. It's going to make your life a lot happier if you like these characters, or at least they intrigue you.

It's going to make your script a lot better, too. So many writers feel compelled to write, say, a *Sopranos* simply because it's the "hot" show. That's great if you have some kind of feel for the show. But if you watch it week after week and keep thinking, Why do people like this? or even Geez, why don't the cops just shoot all these SOBs? you're not going to write a good *Sopranos*, no matter how fine a writer you are.

Remember, it's not enough that your unique voice and vision shine through this script. You need to prove that you can mimic the style and feeling of a show while still letting your unique voice and vision shine through.

What shows do you look forward to? Which world would you like to live in? Which characters would be happiest living in your brain for a few weeks?

Odds are, if you're thinking about trying to become a TV writer, you already know what show you want to spec—you just don't know you know. It's the one you watch every week, and when it's over, you find yourself thinking, That was pretty good, but wouldn't it be cool if . . .

Because just about every great TV episode starts with *Wouldn't it be cool if?*

If you have to force story ideas to come, you've probably chosen the wrong show to spec. There must be another series you watch that generates ideas in your head every time you watch it. That's the one for you; it's that simple.

Almost.

Actually, there are two almosts.

There are some shows that are useless to spec because their format won't allow you to do good work. And there are some that are almost as useless because even if they let you do great work, no one will want to read them.

Without a doubt, the best show to spec is the one you can relate to. That's the one that will allow you to shine as a writer.

Unless it's the kind of show that doesn't allow shining.

You might love *Walker, Texas Ranger*, to cite a recently canceled example. You might want to write about a soft-spoken, high-kicking defender of the American way, a true hero in a land that needs them more than ever.

Don't do it.

The trouble is—and we're trying to keep our own aesthetic judgments out of this—the kind of writing in *Walker* is not considered *good writing* on most other shows. Layered characters? *Walker* likes 'em simple, all good or all bad. Complex plotting? *Walker* likes it straightforward: the bad guys commit a crime and Walker kicks the stuffing out of them. Clever, intricate dialogue? *Walker* doesn't trust the stuff—use what you need for exposition and shut up.

But what if you have a vision—not *Walker* as it is, but *Walker* as it should be? You're going to write a script that delves deep into Walker's character, that explores the nuances of heroism in twenty-first-century America, that probes the contradictions and compromises of a modern Ranger's life. It could be a great, powerful, moving script.

One small problem: It's not a *Walker*.

It's not your job to write the show you think it *should* be; it's your job to write the best possible version of the show that *is*. Writers who try to correct the faults in the series they're writing, to improve on the franchise, to modify the characters, to correct the obvious flaws are never going to be taken seriously. The producer won't be offended—he'll just write you off as an amateur.

By definition, a subtle, nuanced, difficult *Walker* is not a good *Walker*, no matter how inspired the writing is. And just about anyone reading it will know that—even people who don't watch *Walker* have a pretty good idea what it is.

That is, if they'll read it at all.

Keep in mind, the people who are picking scripts to read off the giant stack are hoping to find something they like. And even if we know that there's an equal chance that any two specs will be good or bad, we inevitably gravitate toward shows we know and like.

There is one legitimate reason for that—if we read a *Law & Order: Special Victims Unit* script and find Munch annoying, we know whether he's annoying because that's the way he's supposed to be (good) or because the writer has completely missed his character (bad). But if we're reading a *Sir Arthur Conan Doyle's The Lost World* spec, and the jungle girl in the fur bikini suddenly starts quoting

Rabelais, say, is that the way the show works, or is it a mistake on the writer's part?

Reading a spec from a show you've never seen is a fundamentally frustrating experience. Who are these characters? What are they supposed to be doing? It's difficult to judge the quality of the writing when you don't understand anything that's going on.

When we're running a show, we try to parcel out sample scripts—specs and produced episodes—to people on our staff who know the shows. Lee watches *NYPD Blue* and *CSI*, so he reads those. Bill takes the *Buffys* and *West Wings*. Larry has seen every *X-Files*, and David knows all the late-night and syndicated hours, so he gets those scripts. That way the next reader (if the script passes the first test) can be assured that the spec works *as a spec*. Then the only question becomes, *Is this writer right for us?*

There's also a certain degree of snobbery out there. (We know, you're shocked.) Some people simply will not read scripts—specs or even produced episodes—from syndicated shows. Because of that, agents are unwilling to send them out, or even look at them.

When we were hiring writers for *Martial Law*, which was intended to be a light action-adventure show in the spirit of 1960s series like *It Takes a Thief* and *The Man from U.N.C.L.E.*, we were inundated with specs from *Homicide* and *The Practice*, both of which were far too dark to show that a writer could give us what we needed. When we explained this to agents, they buried us in an avalanche of spec *Ally McBeals* and *Sex and the Citys*—again, not exactly what we were looking for.

Finally, we had to get specific with the agents—send us *Xenas*. Send us *Hercules*. Send us *Buffys*. And there was always a shocked silence on the other end of the phone. *You actually want to read those?* Of course we did—those were series that approximated the tone we were striving to set. We even agreed to look at a couple of produced *Team Knight Rider* episodes. Even so, just about every *Xena* we got was accompanied by an *Ally* or a *Homicide*, just in case we were kidding.

We weren't. The writers we ended up hiring came from *Star Trek: Voyager* and *Hercules* and *La Femme Nikita*.

There are also some commonsense rules to keep in mind when you sit down to choose a spec:

Pick a show that's going to be around for a while. Logic would tell you that it doesn't make any difference if the show you've specced is still on the air. After all, we've all seen *Homicide*; who cares if it was canceled a couple of years ago?

Unfortunately, everyone. For some reason, a spec script of a canceled show is about as welcome as month-old lox. People just don't want to read it.

Do your best to pick a show that's got a few years left on it. And if that show changes substantially—let's say a cast change brings in a replacement for a series regular—it's not a bad idea to update your script. Don't spend your entire life reworking this one spec, but how hard is it to switch the ADA in your *Law & Order*?

Pick a show that isn't going to change dramatically. Remember how much trouble we had trying to figure out *the story* that would work for us on *Baywatch*? Just about every series goes through the same growing pains. That's why it's usually a mistake to spec a first-season show. If the writers on staff haven't figured out how to write the series, odds are you're not going to, either. And even if you beat them to the best possible version of the show, odds are it won't be the same version they come up with, and we know who wins that fight.

Avoid heavily serialized shows, too. Primetime soaps are notoriously bad specs because their characters are in constant flux. You're going to have to pick one particular spot in the story line to set your script, and while you're taking the narrative in one direction, the showrunners will be going somewhere else. By the time your script is out of Kinko's, it's going to feel dated or, worse, just plain wrong. If you're speccing a show that runs long narrative arcs, don't focus on the ongoing story. Write a stand-alone, one that could fit into any season.

Pick a show watched by people in the business. It's going to be a lot easier for everyone involved if the people reading your spec have watched the show you're trying to write for. But how do you know what shows other writers are watching? One simple way is to check out the Emmy nominations—writers nominate their own. (Of course, if four of the five nominated episodes come from *The Sopranos*, as happened one year, this won't do you a lot of good. Unless you want to write a *Sopranos*.) You should also see which shows critics keep talking about; other writers are probably checking them out, too. And finally, look at the ratings. If a drama is in the top ten, odds are other writers are keeping an eye on it.

Break all the rules and do what feels right. Imagine sitting down today and writing a spec *Lou Grant*. Sounds nuts, right? But in the early 1990s one team of sitcom writers found their way onto the highest-rated comedy on TV with a spec *I Love Lucy*. Sure, it was gimmicky, but the novelty caught people's eyes, and probably got their script off the pile well before all the *Cosbys* and *Night Courts* that had stacked up around it. You're taking a bigger chance if you try something this off the wall, but if it works, you're way ahead of everyone else.

Now what do you do with that spec?

You've got to get it to producers. And to do that, you're going to need an agent.

Exercises

- Pick a show, identify its franchise, and write four sample story lines in a paragraph or less each.
- Do the same exercise again.
- Now do the same exercise one more time.
- We'd tell you to do it again, but the point is, you can't do this exercise often enough. To be a TV writer, this exercise has to become second nature, something you instinctively do every time you watch a TV series. Then it's no longer an exercise, it's what you do for a living.

7

The Name Is Morris, William Morris

Most producers will not read a spec script unless it is submitted by an agent.

You probably think that's because we're a close-knit group of elitist jerks who want to hoard all the money and opportunities for ourselves, and agents are just one more gigantic obstacle we've come up with to keep you out.

You're right.

Sort of.

Agents are the first line of defense for us. They read through all the crap to find the very best people, the writers they can make a living on. And the only way an agent is going to make a living is if his clients are talented, professional, and will do a consistently good job for *us*, the producers.

The great thing about this system for us is that the agent has a real motivation to find the best writers out there, saving us the trouble. Because let's face it, elitist jerks like us don't want to work any harder than we have to.

But agents do more than save us extra work. They also protect us. That doesn't mean they'll take a bullet for us or taste our food to make sure it isn't poisoned. But they'll make pretty sure we don't get sued.

We'll give you an example of what we're talking about. Let's say you sent us a script a month ago in which the hero of our show loses his memory. Then you turn on the TV this week, and what do you see on our show? A story about the hero losing his memory. You're going to think we stole it, and sue our asses.

There are a lot of similar themes in stories being developed all the time, and a television professional will understand that. A professional will also understand that the development process is much longer than a month, and that *our* script was probably written long before *yours* showed up in the mail. And a professional will figure that we've probably been pitched fifty amnesia stories, because it's a terrible cliché, right up there with evil doubles and the return of long-lost siblings, that's eventually done on every show.

But without an agent representing you and vouching for you, we have no assurance that you are indeed a professional.

It is a very litigious business, and if an agent sends you to us, he or she is guaranteeing your professionalism. An agent will explain to his or her clients that for every episode of *The District* that airs there are five others in development that didn't or haven't yet. One of those stories may be just like yours.

Enough about what the agent does for us. What does he do for you?

He gets you in our door. He gets you work.

If he's any good, he's got contacts at all the studios and networks, he has good relationships with successful producers, and he knows what shows are out there, and which ones are about to get cancelled.

He'll know where there are script assignments available and which producers are most likely to respond to your writing. He'll introduce development executives to your work so that they will recommend you for projects. And he'll help you shape a career by advising you on which work to accept and which offers to reject.

He will fight for you, negotiate the hopelessly complex contracts, and, during those inevitable periods of unemployment, reassure you that your career isn't over.

So where can you find an agent?

We could write a book on that, but we won't, because there are already plenty of them out there, filled with good advice and strategies for snaring the right representation.

But we'll give you two places to start.

The first thing you should do is talk to all your friends in the business.

Wait a minute. How do you get friends in the business if you *aren't even in the damn business yet?*

Why did you think we recommended taking some screenwriting courses? It wasn't just to learn how to write a script.

If you're a likeable person, and reasonably social, you'll make some friends in those classes and workshops, and odds are that one or two of them might break into the business before you do. And they'll become your friends in the business.

We are always amazed at just how many people we know in TV who were people we knew *before* we were in TV.

Do they help us get work? All the time, even now.

The other thing you can do to find an agent is call the Writers Guild of America. For the price of a stamp, they will send you a list of agents who have signed the WGA Agency Agreement. What sets these agents apart from all the others is that they meet the standards of conduct and professionalism set and maintained by the Guild. The agents have also consented to negotiate agreements that assure writers of, at the very least, the rights and minimum fees established by the overall contract the Guild negotiated with the studios and networks.

That doesn't mean that these agents will sign you, but at least you'll know you're dealing with reputable professionals, not one of the legions of scumbags out there who say they are agents and aren't.

When you're struggling to get your foot in the door, searching for an agent sometimes becomes an all-encompassing task. Talk to aspiring writers, check out message headings in chat groups on the Internet; the same question keeps coming up—how do I find an agent? Unfortunately, people rarely ask a more important question:

"What do I want from an agent?"

Maybe the answer seems too obvious—you want someone peddling your scripts around town. You want someone who can get you read.

But any reputable agent, and a lot who aren't, can get you read. When we're hiring writers, we take calls from all sorts of agencies. Are we faster to pick up the phone when it's CAA or William Morris instead of the Bernie Grinchluck Agency? Maybe you'll be surprised to hear this—and maybe you won't want to believe it—but our answer is no.

Which agent do we talk to first when we're looking for writers? Obviously, our own. We could give you a lot of rationalizations about how he understands our tastes and needs better than any other agent could, but that's not the reason we take his calls first.

We take his calls because we assume he's calling about *us*. And then we're stuck listening to him pitch us his other clients.

Next on the list come agents we have relationships with. That doesn't mean we go to dinner dances with them, or hang out at Starbucks, or even talk more than a couple times a year. Usually these are agents who represent other writers we've hired, or directors we use, agents we've done business with in the past.

After that, we return calls from the guys pitching writers we've heard of. We may be interested in their clients or not, but either way, this is going to be a short conversation—"Sure, we'll read her" or "Sorry, there's no chance we'll ever hire this guy."

And last come agents we don't know who are pitching writers we've never heard of. Doesn't matter whether the agency is big or small, these calls get bumped to the end of the day, but it's not because we're prejudiced against hiring their clients—it's just that these conversations can go on for a long time, as the agent pitches client after client, trying to find a good match.

So if access isn't the issue, how do you know what agent is right for you?

When you're first starting out, it's hard to tell. You want someone pushing your scripts, and it feels like you can't afford to be choosy about who that is. The fact is, you can't afford not to be.

Do you want a giant powerhouse agency or a small boutique? The big houses represent lots of working writers, which means they have lots of clients to nag into reading your work. But it also means they have a lot of other people to service before they get around to you, and every one of those other writers is going to bring more money into the agency than the struggling newcomer.

A boutique agency can offer more personalized representation, but the trade-off is that there may be doors they can't open, or jobs available that they don't even know about.

When we first started out, we had what we thought was the best of both worlds. We teamed up with a young woman in the last stages of the trainees' program at what we'll call the Really Mammoth Agency (RMA). She was plugged into all the inside information that comes into a place like RMA, she had a fleet of experienced agents advising her, and she was really hungry. It was this young woman—let's call her Amy—who advised us to write the *Spenser: For Hire* spec, it was Amy who got it to the studio, it was Amy who kept it alive over there. And when Bill Yates picked our script off that slush pile, we became professional TV writers at the same time Amy became a full-fledged agent.

We were in the best position we could ever hope for at the agency—we were our agent's star clients. Amy devoted lots of thought and time to figuring out where we should be going in our careers. She studied the pilots for the upcoming season to find a show, and a showrunner, that would be perfect for us.

The show she finally chose was *Murphy's Law,* a new romantic comedy mystery series starring George Segal and run by Michael Gleason. Amy figured that our style and sense of humor were similar to Michael's, so that we could do the job the way he'd want. And on his last series, *Remington Steele,* Michael had turned out a staff of writers who went on to be stars—Brad Kern, John Wirth, Jeff Melvoin, Lee David Zlotoff, and Glenn Gordon Caron. (If you don't know these names, you're not spending enough time watching credits.)

We're forever grateful to Amy for setting us up on *Murphy's Law.* It was indeed the perfect place for us. The show was a joy to write, playing exactly into our strengths; we were allowed more input into the production than we've had in some producing jobs; and, most importantly, Michael and supervising producer Ernie Wallengren became our lifelong friends

Unfortunately, the rest of the world didn't share our enthusiasm for *Murphy's Law.* We shot thirteen episodes, aired maybe eleven of them, and were out of work.

That's when things started to go bad at RMA. The next season, Amy didn't spend quite so much time trying to figure out the next best move for our career. She did get us a job, but hardly one suited to our talents. It was a straightforward, unimaginative cop show, essentially the *Walker, Texas Ranger* of its day. Even if we had thrived there, it wasn't going to do much for us besides pay the bills, as the scripts they turned out didn't feature the kind of writing that builds careers. We were getting paid (and we certainly weren't complaining about that at the time), but we had put our future on hold.

Was Amy wrong to put us on this show? It's hard to say. We were hungry for work, and jumped at it when it came along. We'll never blame an agent for getting us a job.

But there were questions that should have been asked, and never were: How does this job fit into our long-term goals? Will this show help us, by getting us into a studio that produces lots of action shows, or will it type us as schlockmeisters? If we do take this job, what can we do at the same time to keep career momentum alive?

Unfortunately, those questions never got asked. Once we were working, we never heard from Amy, or from anyone else at the agency. They had taken care of us, and now they could move on to other clients.

Technically, Amy had done her job by getting us onto this cop show. But she'd risked our future to satisfy our immediate needs.

It's easy to make Amy and the agency into the bad guys of this story—they were the ones who weren't doing their jobs. But the fact is, we're as much to blame as they were. When Amy told us about the job, we never stopped to ask, "Is this right for us?" or "How will this further our long-term career goals?" We asked the one question every writer asks his agent: *"How much?"*

We were content to let our agents think about our futures. That's something we soon learned is a major mistake.

Ideally, writer and agent should be partners, working together to design and build the writer's career. There's no way to predict exactly what opportunities are going to come along, or what disasters will strike along the way, but if the two of you have worked out a plan in advance, at least you have a better idea how to deal with whatever happens. But agents have lots of clients to service, and if you stop calling once you've got a job, they'll assume you're happy and start working for the next guy on the list.

If you want this kind of partnership with your agent, you can't sit back and wait for it to happen. It's your career. It's your move.

Sometimes that move means jumping to another agency. That can be a lot harder than it sounds, especially if you've had a good personal relationship with your agent for a long time.

What you have to remember is that no matter how personally close you feel to your agent, underneath it all, this is a business relationship, not a friendship.

We learned that lesson the hard way. After Amy set us up at the cop show, RMA seemed to lose interest in us. When we were starting on *Murphy's Law,* we were the hot new kids, full of talent and promise. But now we'd gone from a flop show to a crummy minor hit. Maybe we weren't such a good bet after all. And when Amy left the agency on maternity leave, there was no one to look out for us. We couldn't even get a phone call returned. We knew we had to leave.

But then Amy came back from her leave, and the decision got much harder. She pleaded with us to stay, and promised us that things would change at RMA. Although we knew we should find a new agency, we let our personal feelings overrule our brains. Not surprisingly, after a two-month honeymoon, things were once again as bad as they had ever been at RMA. But this time we were spared the emotional roller coaster. RMA merged with another big firm, and Amy was laid off, leaving us no reason to stay.

The relationship between client and agent is a strange one. Essentially, he works for you, but since you depend on him to get you a job, it often feels like it's the other way around. It's going to be up to you to decide what kind of relationship you want with your agent—do you want someone who will micromanage your life to the extent that they're picking out the clothes you'll wear to meetings, as some of our friends do? Or could you be happy, as some of our other friends are, with a team of representatives so impersonal you can only think of them as "the replicants"?

Every relationship is different, and what's ideal for one writer is going to be a nightmare for three others. The best advice we can give is to follow your gut.

That's how we chose our current agent. When we were looking, we met with everybody, big and small. One guy looked at our résumé and announced he'd have to white out half the credits, because the jobs we'd done were too diverse, making it too hard to push an image for us. Another guy promised we'd be running three shows in a year, but couldn't quite seem to remember exactly who we were.

The agent we finally signed with wasn't the biggest or the most prestigious. But he did say the words that no one else we met with came close to. When we asked why he wanted to represent us, he said, "I really like your writing." That's what sold it for us. Who knows what's going to make the sale for you?

Exercises

- Call the WGA and get the list of signatory agents. But don't call the agents yet, because you don't have a spec ready. But at least you will have taken the first, obligatory step.
- Read *Variety* and start comparing the names of agents mentioned in all those articles about deals for TV writers with the names on your signatory list. Pretty soon, you'll have a list of the best agents in TV . . . or at least those who are getting their clients jobs.

8

The Pitch

Congratulations. Your spec really was as good as you thought it was. It's landed you an agent, and now that agent has scored you a meeting with the executive producer of a TV show.

You finally got in the door.

Everybody always says that's the hardest part. Well, we're here to tell you they're wrong.

The hardest part is about to begin.

Everything else you've done up until now has been alone, in the darkness and comfort of your home or office. You've watched some TV, you've done some reading, you've written a couple of scripts, you've received a few rejections (okay, lots of them, but who's counting?).

But the fact is, you've been sheltered. It's your *work* that's been out there working, and getting rejected, while you've been at home screwing around.

You, yourself, in the flesh, haven't been on the line yet.

Now you will be.

It doesn't matter now how good your spec script was. It almost doesn't matter how good your ideas are. What is going to be judged now is *you*. The producer already likes your writing, now he's going to found out if he likes you, the way you think, and the way you work with others.

A pitch is an audition. You are auditioning for a script, and the chance to work with the writing staff of the show, in almost the same way an actor auditions for a role, only the material you'll be performing isn't being supplied to you, it's your own.

You're going to find yourself ushered into a room, maybe with the executive producer, more likely with a supervising producer or even someone further down the hierarchy. (There are rules about this, by the way. Officially, you can only be asked to pitch to someone with the power to say yes. But even if you're meeting with a staff writer, what are you going to do? File a grievance? Take what they give you.) Sometimes you'll be pitching to an entire writing staff.

But no matter how many people are in the room, there's one thing they all have in common—not one of them wants to be there.

It's nothing personal. After all, your script has convinced at least one of them that you can do some good for the show. But everybody in that room has at least three other things they need to be doing: writing a script, cracking a story, casting a show, attending a production meeting, talking to the network. And they've all got homes they'd like to see again before midnight. You are one more thing keeping them from realizing that dream.

So you've got about two minutes to win them over.

Make no mistake about it, this is a job interview. Dress accordingly. Just because the guys you'll be meeting may be in jeans and T-shirts doesn't mean you should be. They've already got the job, they've earned the right to dress any way they want. You haven't yet. That doesn't mean you have to wear a three-piece suit or a formal dress, but you should look nice.

You'd think that would be common sense and would go without saying, but you'd be surprised how many people have come into our offices dressed in jeans and ratty tennis shoes, effecting an air of casual nonchalance, trying to show us how L.A. casual they can be, how cool and plugged-in they are. What it actually says is that I have no respect for you and I couldn't care less whether I get this job or not.

You'll inevitably spend the first few minutes with casual small talk, the "getting to know you" part of the meeting. But no matter how friendly the producers are or how much they encourage you to talk, they really don't want to hear your entire life story. Be brief. Remember, they all want to be somewhere else. As relaxed as a good producer might try to make you feel, they really don't have much time and really appreciate it if you don't ramble on forever with all your favorite anecdotes about getting into the business.

After the small talk, the producer will say something like, "So, what do you have for me today?" and that's your cue. You're on.

We know what you're thinking: Wait a minute, I'm a writer, not a performer. If I wanted to act, I wouldn't be reading this book.

Being a successful TV writer is as much about your people skills and your ability to sell yourself, as it is about your writing. There are a lot of mediocre writers out there with fabulous careers because of their terrific people skills: they are good in a room and know how to work well with producers, agents, and executives.

If that's too daunting for you, put down this book and buy one on how to be a novelist. An author can work at home, send his work out, and wait for the contracts and checks to show up in his mailbox. A TV writer can't. Television is a collaborative medium, and the pitch meeting is the first opportunity a producer has to see your ability to express your ideas and how you work with others.

You should come in the door with three solid ideas for the show, and maybe a half dozen half-baked notions for stories. Often, if your solid ideas get shot down, one of your vague ideas will get a producer going and you'll walk out of the room with a story assignment.

But we're getting ahead of ourselves. Let's go back to the pitch.

The most important thing is to be entertaining, upbeat, and enthusiastic. You are trying to talk the producer into essentially writing you a check for $27,000, the WGA minimum for a teleplay. It's up to you to convince him your story is worth it. If you go in unexcited by the story, how do you expect the producer to have any enthusiasm?

Unless the producer interrupts you and asks for specifics, present only the general, broad strokes of your story. You might start with the teaser, then launch into the major character arcs and the act breaks. Don't focus on the mundane details. The producer doesn't want to know every scene in every act, at least not yet.

A good rule of thumb is to tell your story the way you would describe a great, or even awful, movie you saw last night to a friend. Think about it. When you describe a movie, you don't give every detail, you give a sense of what the movie was about, then you jump right to the big stuff that you either really liked or really hated.

Let's say you saw *The Full Monty* and wanted to tell your friend about it. You might say: "I saw this great movie last night. There are these unemployed steelworkers who can't get a job, so to make a buck, they become strippers—but they've all got bodies like mine."

That's a pitch. You don't start out with "There's this town in England and the economy is real bad. All the factories are closing. People are out of work. There are these guys, one of them is divorced, and he's having a hard time. And he has this other friend, who is also out of work, and. . . ."

No, you get right into it. You go to the heart of the story and then, if necessary, give up the details. You wait for your friend, or in this case the producer, to ask what happens next.

That question, "What happens next?" is the sound of success. When we say that, you know we're interested and that you have a good shot of making a sale.

A lot of good writers come into our office and pitch good stories very badly. Actually, we're giving them the benefit of the doubt here. We'll never know if they are good stories, because by the time the writer gets to the good part, we're already hoping an earthquake will strike and save us from having to listen to another word.

A bad writer will come in and start a pitch like this: "I've got a terrific story for you. A patient comes into the hospital, his name is Fred. He comes into the hospital and . . . did I mention he's got this dog? Let me go back. His name is Fred and he has this dog and he comes into the hospital. His dog is a terrier, or a retriever. He, the patient, comes into the hospital because he found this dead woman in his house. Did I mention the dog's name is Irving? Let me go back."

Or they tell every single beat of the story.

"Joe comes into the hospital and sees Dr. Sloan. He says, 'Hello, Dr. Sloan.' The doctor says, 'Hello, Joe.' Dr. Sloan is wearing a white lab coat and there's a coffee stain on his lapel. It is from decaffeinated coffee with two spoonfuls of sugar. . . ."

Forty-five minutes later, when they finally get around to what the story is about, you've already decided never to work with this writer, no matter how good his story might be, because his major talent is actually sucking all the oxygen out of a room, along with your soul.

What we want is a writer to come in and say, "Have I got a story for you. Dr. Bentley is doing an autopsy and it's late, late at night, and she's standing over the body and she is saying the guy died with a bullet wound to the head and he bled out this way, all that technical stuff. Suddenly the dead body sits up, grabs her by the throat, and strangles her until she is unconscious. The corpse skulks out of the room, leaving a trail of blood."

And we're thinking: What happens next? How come the guy isn't dead if he had a bullet in his head? Is Dr. Bentley going to survive? Where is that guy going? What does he want?

Granted, there isn't a character hook yet, but if you're a good writer, there will be before the story is over.

Or someone comes into the office and says, "Have I got a story for you. Dr. Sloan is sitting at night in front of his computer, surfing the web, and gets one of those voyeuristic web sites where the camera is on in a person's dorm room twenty-four hours a day. Dr. Sloan is watching some college kid sitting there eating Doritos when suddenly a guy comes in with an ax and whacks the kid's head off. Mark has just witnessed a murder on his laptop, what's he going to do?"

That's a terrific hook. It invites the producer to ask, "What happens next?"

You don't need to start a pitch with the hook. Sometimes it's best to begin with the story's central conflict—"We all know how Buffy hates vampires—what would happen if she *became* a vampire? That's what this story is about, and it begins on a dark and stormy night. . . ."

There's a risk to this kind of pitch, though. If the producers have already considered this kind of conflict and have either rejected it or are actively developing it, they're going to cut you off before you can get into your narrative. You've lost your chance to show them how well you can craft a story. With a different kind of pitch, you might be able to hook them before they realize there's a problem and convince them to take your idea in a different direction.

But there's more to a pitch and more to making a sale than a clever idea that's enthusiastically and entertainingly presented.

A producer also wants to see how you work with others and how you think on your feet. Just because you have a good idea, and a producer is intrigued by it, doesn't mean you're finished with your pitch. Often a producer will want to shape an idea right there in the room. That shaping might come in the form of questions.

The producer might say, "You know we did something very similar to that last season, but what if we changed it? What if instead of being about a killer bug it is about a killer dog? What if instead of a hurricane it's an earthquake? What if Uncle Joe is murdered instead of the mailman?"

You get the idea.

The important thing is, don't be married to what you pitch. Be prepared to make changes to satisfy the producer, even if you think they're wrong. You aren't there to protect the artistic integrity of your idea. You're there to sell an idea that works for the producer's show.

Your job when the producer poses one of those questions is not to defend your idea, but to make it work, or, at the very least, to entertain the suggestion and see how it plays and changes the elements of the story the producer likes.

You can't cringe and say, "No, that is not my vision," or "That screws up everything." You have to roll with it, and if it does screw up everything, you have to explain why it does. Or you have just talked yourself out of $27,000. Believe it or not, we see writers do this all the time.

No matter what happens in the room, you can't get mad. Believe it or not, there are some producers out there who are not very nice people. And there are some who are usually nice, but happen to be in a particularly bad mood at the time you're trying to sell them a story. And they may take it out on you.

Many years ago, we had been brought in to pitch on a new show by our friends, who were story editors. We were taken to the supervising producer and after the obligatory chitchat launched into our first story.

We were halfway through when the supervising producer got up without saying a word and walked to the office door. Then he smiled sweetly and said, "You keep pitching—I'm going to the bathroom to throw up."

It was outrageously offensive. In fact, it was probably deliberately provocative. We would have been justified in storming out of there. But while that might have left us feeling morally righteous, it would also have left us feeling unemployed. So we smiled just as sweetly, said something like "Guess you don't like that one," and moved on to our next story.

And yes, we got an assignment.

It is the producer's show. You are there to perform a service. You are like a handyman who has been hired to fix a door in their house. They ask you to come in and fix a story for them, to give them an episode. Your job is to do what they ask.

Look at it another way. You are a contractor; the series is their house. You may know how to remodel it, but the client has to live there. They are going to have suggestions, and they are going to give you input. Your ability to be flexible will decide whether you get the job or not.

Sometimes a story will take a life of its own in the room and you will know before you leave if you have sold it or not. Other times, a producer will be taking seven pitches in a day and will want to think about how the stories he's heard fit into the overall scheme of what he or she wants to do with the show for the season.

No matter what, whether you think you've sold a story or not, thank the producer for his time and leave a good impression and a **leave-behind.**

Although the producer, or one of his assistants will undoubtedly be taking notes during your pitch, you don't want to trust someone else's note-taking skills to capture the astonishing brilliance of your idea. You should take on that responsibility yourself. That is where the leave-behind, the written synopsis of your idea, comes in. Not the whole story, one page tops, three paragraphs with the beginning, middle, and end, like jacket copy on a book. Punchy, well written, it really gives the flavor of the episode we've pitched.

You want them to be able to read the leave-behind long after you've left and get the feel, and the excitement, of the pitch all over again, to remember why they liked the story and why they have to hire you.

Some people are nervous about leave-behinds; they're afraid it makes it easier for producers to steal their ideas.

It's an unfounded fear.

The reason producers hire freelancers is so that we don't have to write another episode. A great idea and a talented freelancer to write it are a godsend. But on a more practical level, it's cheaper for us to buy your story than to steal it. Besides, it's not our money. If you come in and say you have a great idea for a story, why wouldn't we buy it? It's not money out of our pockets, and it certainly is cheaper than getting sued. So even if we like your idea and we don't think you can write it, we will still buy it from you and simply hire someone else (or a member of our staff) to write it.

We can think of very, very few cases of plagiarism in the TV business. But if you're worried about it anyway, you can always register your ideas with the Writers Guild of America for a small fee.

So now you have an idea of *how* you're going to pitch. That still leaves an important question: How do you know *what* to pitch?

Exercises

- Practice telling friends about the movie you saw last weekend or the show you watched last night. Pay attention to their reactions. How long do they stay interested? When do they get bored? At what point do they either fall asleep or run screaming out of the room? By doing this, you can hone the way you tell the story. Keep asking yourself how you can make your story more interesting. Are there details you should leave out? Plot points that don't matter? How about the way you tell the story? Are you talking too quickly? Too slowly? Are you energetic, or low-key? Which approach works best for you?
- Now try pitching to your friends those four spec ideas you came up with in Chapter 6 using the same technique.

9

How to Read the Producer's Mind

If you're invited to come in and pitch a show, you will be sent some material to help you prepare. You'll probably get a couple episodes on tape, a few scripts, a list of stories in development, and perhaps even a copy of their bible. And we don't mean the Holy Bible, unless, perhaps, you're writing for *Seventh Heaven*. A bible is the TV term for a show's "writers' guidelines" (and we've included copies of our guidelines from *Diagnosis Murder* and *Martial Law* in the appendixes as examples).

All that is nice and very helpful, but the key to making the sale, as it is in any business, is getting in the customers' heads and figuring out what they want, even if they don't know yet that they want it. But unlike any other business, your customers—the producers—make it easy for you to read their minds.

It doesn't take a crystal ball or psychic powers. All it takes is sixty seconds in front of a TV set. All you have to do is watch the main title sequence.

You're thinking, So what? A main title is just a stupid song and some visuals, right?

It's much more than that.

The main title for a series can cost anywhere from forty to one hundred thousand dollars and usually is made up of ten or twelve shots pulled from the show.

Think about that. Out of all the episodes, out of thousands of feet of film, they choose only ten or twelve shots.

You think that's easy? It's not. A lot of thought goes into the selection of those shots. Why did they pick those images? What were the producers trying to say? Why did they pick that theme music or those lyrics? What information were they trying to convey?

Main titles are created to introduce the audience to the show they are about to see. But for the writer, there is much more information to be gleaned. It is a chance to read the mind of the executive producer. How does he perceive the show? How does he perceive the characters? How does he perceive the tone? What kinds of stories does he want to tell? Most main title sequences will answer all those questions and more.

There are basically three different kinds of main title sequences: **format** sequences, which actually tell you in narration and in writing what the show is about; **mood** sequences, which convey the type of feeling and tone they are going for; and **character** sequences, which delineate who the characters are and how they interact. Many main titles are combinations of these three sequences.

Since TV changes so fast, we've chosen some examples from some established series you probably know very well and, if not, can easily find in reruns.

Hunter

This is a classic character sequence.

The writers' bible for *Hunter* was about thirty pages long, but freelancers didn't have to read it. Everything you needed to know about the show was right there in the main title.

Before we sold our first script to *Hunter* we watched that main title sequence about fifty times, because they did over 100 episodes of that show and from those chose just a dozen shots. Why? What emphasis did they put where?

You know it's a hard action show from the music and the stunts. You also know that every single story has got to be driven by Hunter. You will notice Hunter never opens a door. He kicks it open. He doesn't let people get in his way. He knocks them down and shoots.

This is a man who is always moving forward. So you know your stories have to have Hunter at the core and they've got to move. He's pushing the story. He's not passive. Things don't happen to him, *he* happens *to them*.

You know Hunter is a cop and you know that is important to him. You also know he's a loner and he thinks he is God. You will notice the only things bigger than Hunter in the main title sequence are his gun and his badge. You know right away that this man is totally wrapped up in being a cop and that the only things that are more important to him than himself are his badge and his gun.

You also saw that his captain was a peripheral character. He had two shots. So you know not to have big scenes with that character; he's not important.

In the first few seasons of the show, Hunter was seen in lots of shots with his partner, Sergeant McCall (Stephane Kramer). But in later seasons, they were rarely in the same shot together. And when you did see her, she wasn't doing the action stuff, she was seen on the phone or interviewing people. The change in their relationship that's reflected in the main titles should tell you that the show wasn't about their partnership any more, and that stories should be much more focused on Hunter as a lone action hero, with McCall handling all the plot stuff.

There were only two or three shots that had any kind of humor in them, but it was humor that went against Hunter's cynicism. You saw him looking at a baby. You saw him with strippers. You saw him lying on a vibrating bed. So you know that the humor in *Hunter* comes from putting this rigid man in situations where his rigidity can be made fun of or he will feel awkward because of his rigidity. Put him with babies, put him with strippers, and put him in an X-rated motel room with a vibrating bed. Put him in situations where that rigidity gets tested.

The last shot you see is Hunter standing over the city. The city is his. He sees it as his job to protect and take care of the city.

Some main title sequences don't force you to read between the lines. Some come right out and tell you what the show is. Here is one of them.

Law & Order

This is a classic format sequence, which begins with a black screen and the following narration:

> In the criminal justice system the people are represented by two separate yet equally important groups: the police who investigate crimes and the district attorneys who prosecute the offenders. These are their stories.

Law & Order's franchise is unique. A group of police detectives solve a crime in the first half and a group of DAs prosecute the offenders in the second. These are your four acts. They've just told you. It doesn't get any clearer than that.

Hunter's main title sequence was all about his character. There is no character at all in the *Law & Order* title sequence. In fact, you only see the cast in still photos. What you do see are photos of procedure, of courtrooms, of people huddling, of people in jail, of the minutiae of the law. What they are telling you is that the characters don't matter—it is the process that we care about.

As you think about a story for *Law & Order*, you can tell it has to be about the process, about a crime and how it is prosecuted and what the twists are. Don't try an episode in which one of the cops is concerned that his aunt is being charged with a crime she didn't commit. That is not the franchise.

Walker, Texas Ranger

This is a character and format sequence. *Walker*'s main title features Chuck Norris, the star of the show, singing a song against the backdrop of big action sequences. Chuck sings about the omnipotence of the mighty Texas Ranger who, like a gun-toting Santa Claus, is always watching you, knows if you've been bad or good, and will be right there to catch you if you commit a crime.

Without even seeing the main title sequence, without even

reading a script, you know that this guy is a Texas Ranger and he is the center of every story. He's a man of action.

And as if the lyrics of the title song aren't big enough clues, Walker himself sings it, and his face is in almost every single shot.

So you know that Walker, just like Hunter, is the center of every story. You also know that action and physical violence are a major part of the show. And you know that he's always going to be one step ahead of the bad guys.

We have only watched a few episodes of *Walker*, for a crossover episode we did on *Martial Law*, but we can tell you that from just watching the title sequence and listening to that horrible song, he never makes a mistake. He is the nicest guy on earth, the best fighter on earth, and the best cop. He's almost superhuman.

Criminals are either good or bad. There is no in between. And Walker, like Santa Claus, omnisciently knows which is which.

Chuck is the star and the executive producer and he sings the song. What more do you need to know about what a *Walker* story should be?

The X-Files

This is a mood and format sequence. The main title sequence remained unchanged until David Duchovny left, which alone should tell you something about how important the sequence is to the producers in stating what the show is about (and the fact that the show tanked after Duchovny left should tell you how much more important characters are to viewers than the stories).

First of all, you know right away that the format is science fiction, horror, and fantasy. You know that the show is scary. That means your stories also better have a scare in them.

You can also tell from the main title sequence that the style and tone—and the feelings they evoke—are very, very important, more so than the minutiae of the story. That main title is all about creating a feeling in you before the show even begins.

You also know right away that this is a show about two FBI

agents who investigate paranormal activity because we are actually shown their FBI IDs. The title sequence tells you in big print exactly what they investigate and suggests that it involves conspiracies about which the government denies all knowledge.

The music is creepy and distant. You know it's not a show that is going to be fun and games. There is not a lot of humor and high jinks. It's about government conspiracies and the supernatural.

So you know the tone your story has to have. You know the two of them have to be at the center of it. You know that there had better be some scares in it. You never have to watch an episode of *The X-Files* to know all of that—you just have to watch the main title.

CSI: Crime Scene Investigation

The title alone should tell you a lot. But beyond that, the brilliant main title sequence does an exceptional job selling the mood and format of the series.

Part of the brilliance of the main title sequence is that it goes against everything we've been taught about what is dramatic (not coincidentally, much like the show itself). While other main titles are full of slickly edited explosions, car chases, amazing stunts, and scenes of conflict, this one features shots of evidence being collected and analyzed.

How exciting can looking at a piece of lint under a microscope be? Very exciting, judging by the way these shots are cut into the main title, which also tells you something about how the producers approach story. The forensics are the story.

We see quick shots of crime scene tape, fingerprints, broken glass, drops of blood, a strand of hair, a bullet moving through water, a guy setting his equipment case down beside a body. Here the mundane is edited like a martial arts sequence.

The producers could have included a shot of cops kicking down doors, buildings exploding, moments that have happened during the course of the series. But those action-packed shots aren't in the main title. Why? Because while those were exciting moments in the show, they aren't what the *series* is about. It's a show about forensics.

Look at the way the characters are introduced as compared to, say, in the main titles of any other show. No attempt is made to reveal character, to tell us who they are as people, or even to make them look particularly heroic or attractive. Each character is introduced peering at some tiny piece of evidence under a microscope or between a pair of tweezers, squinting at some computer printout, crouching over a corpse, or aiming a flashlight into a dark corner. Because, like *Law & Order*, this isn't a show about the characters. It's a show about forensics.

The series also takes place in Las Vegas, but with the exception of two quick night shots of the city, you don't see the typical glittering footage you'd expect of the Strip, showgirls dancing, and roulette wheels spinning. Why? Because this isn't a show about Las Vegas. It's a show about forensics.

And if the visuals didn't pound home the point hard enough, let's consider the theme song, the Who's "Who Are You?" The cost of using that song every week is probably larger than the national debt of several third world countries, so it's obviously important to the producers. The fact that it's a classic, and catchy, song by a legendary rock group doesn't hurt. It sticks in your head. In fact, it was probably there long before *CSI* came along. That alone would probably be worth the hefty price tag. But what really makes this song worth every penny is the simple lyric: *Who are you? Who? Who? I really want to know.* That lyric is repeated again and again over the visuals, combining with them to send you a message you'd have to be deaf and blind not to get.

It's a show about forensics.

The producers don't care about car chases, or explosions, or gunfights. They don't care about romance, sex, and witty repartee. They aren't particularly interested in moving character drama, either. They care about cool forensics and intricate mysteries.

You'll notice that just about every scene in the main title was either shot at night or in a darkened room, which should also tell you something about the mood. This is not a bright and cheery show. In fact, just about the only light you see is coming from flashlights. What are they saying? That the stories and the characters move in the shadows.

The title of the show is *Crime Scene Investigation*. The visuals are only about evidence collection and analysis. The song asks over and over again, *Who are you?* Someone who has never seen a single episode of *CSI*, someone who doesn't even speak or read English, could watch the main titles and tell you what the show is about and what the center of each story is.

This is a perfect main title, and about as clear an indication as you could ever get into how the producers see their own show.

So as you begin to craft your stories, keep the main titles of the show you're pitching to in mind. Does your story fulfill what the main title promises? If it doesn't, you're pitching the wrong stories.

Exercise

- Isn't it obvious what we're going to ask you to do? Videotape several main title sequences. Break the sequences down into shots. Now explain why every shot is in the main title and what it is meant to convey.

10

What to Pitch

Before you can start to craft a story for a series, you have to understand what elements that story *must* contain. You have to ask yourself, as we explained in the previous chapter, what makes it a *West Wing*, a *Judging Amy*, or a *Monk*? But that's only the first step. You then have to ask yourself what's going to make your story *special*. What's going to make your script a great *West Wing*, *Judging Amy*, or *Monk*?

If it's a detective show, don't think about the case. If it's an occult show, don't think about the monster. If it's a medical show, don't think about the illness.

So what *should* you be thinking about?

Conflict.

Conflict is the sparks that fly when people encounter obstacles to their goals, even when those barriers exist only within themselves. It is the essence, the soul, of drama.

Each series approaches conflict in a different way. Some concentrate on the conflicts between the regular characters. Others examine the internal, moral, and psychological conflicts within an individual character. Still others do a little of both, but highlight the conflicts that arise when characters team up to overcome a shared obstacle or achieve a common goal.

Whatever story you decide to pitch must reflect the conflicts within the series, as well as the simple conflicts that make a good story on *any* series.

Ask yourself some important questions about the show. Who are the characters? What are their relationships? What aspects of those relationships haven't been explored in past episodes? What is the series *really* about, beyond the legal issues, medical treatments, alien worlds, and mythical creatures?

Your story should be character-based and conflict-driven, a combination that will excite producers the most. If you can explore their main character in a way that they haven't—without bringing in his long-lost brother or child he never knew he had—they'll be thrilled.

To create a story like this, start by asking yourself: How do my characters get involved in this story? What is at stake for them? How is this different from the story we told last week?

No one remembers the cases Jim Rockford took on, but they remember the trouble he got into. The best *Rockford Files* episodes always had Rockford personally involved in the case he was investigating, beyond just solving his client's problem. Like the one where Rockford comes back from a Hawaiian vacation and two thugs ambush him in his trailer and beat him up with the warning, "Stay off the Smith case." Jim hasn't been on a case, he's been on vacation. He has no idea who Smith is. But thugs keep showing up and trashing him and threatening him anyway. It turns out that while he was gone, his mechanic was driving around in his Firebird, taking on cases and telling everybody he's Jim Rockford, getting poor Rockford into a hell of a mess. And that's the fun of the episode. No one remembers what the Smith case was about (or, to be honest, if it was even called "the Smith case," which it probably wasn't). What we remember is the predicament Rockford was in.

That's the conflict that drives the episode. That's the character challenge that captivates viewers. That's the kind of story you should be pitching.

The conflict in *The X-Files* is not what monster or conspiracy Mulder and Scully tackle that week. The conflict is how that monster or conspiracy affects them individually, their relationship, and their long-term goals. The episodes you remember most are the ones that stretched the limits of Mulder and Scully's relationship, that explored the mythology of the series.

Why?

Because it's the characters you care about, not the stories.

That doesn't mean you should tell lousy stories, but that the characters come first.

After Bill Yates bought our spec, we made our first freelance sale to *Spenser: For Hire* by exploring an aspect of the detective's character that hadn't been dealt with before.

In the series, even more than in the books, Spenser always jumped into cases without any concern whatsoever about getting paid. He was this noble knight, good to the core and so full of integrity you wanted to vomit. We decided to explore that aspect of his character.

In our story, Spenser comes back to his office after two days on a stakeout. He hasn't slept in twenty-four hours. He pours himself a cup of coffee and looks out the window, and there is a woman standing on the ledge of the next building. Before he can do anything, she jumps and there's nothing Spenser can do to help her. Now Spenser becomes obsessed with finding out why she jumped.

Except that it's none of his damned business and everyone keeps telling him so, but he can't sleep until he finds out why this woman wanted to take her own life. And because he can't sleep, he begins to deteriorate physically and mentally. The episode became an exploration of why Spenser does what he does, and the price he pays for it.

Why does it matter to him why a complete stranger jumps off a building? No one has hired him, no one has asked for his help, so what is he doing there?

We did tell a crime story in there, but what hooked the producers was, "Yeah, why does Spenser do all of this? What is this twisted sense of morality he has that he thinks he has to solve everybody's problems?"

That really excited them.

But it was a good pitch for another reason. It was a story that was tailor-made for *Spenser: For Hire*. It couldn't be told, for example, on *The Rockford Files*, a series that had a whole different tone. If we'd gone in to see *Rockford Files* producer Steve Cannell and said, "Rockford sees a woman jump off a ledge and becomes obsessed with finding out why," Steve would have said, "Where is the money in it for Rockford? What does he care? That's not our show." And Steve would have been right.

Coming up with fresh stories and new conflicts for shows that have been on the air for a long time is an especially difficult challenge, but one that offers unique opportunities for freelancers. You can look at the series with a fresh eye, from the outside, something producers who have been involved in dozens of episodes of the show can not. And if you pull it off, you stand a good chance of landing multiple assignments or a staff job.

We went in to pitch *Matlock* during its last year or so on the air. It had already been on for a century and the executive producer was eager for fresh ideas. We were between series, so we figured, why not?

We gave it some thought. What kind of story could we tell that would explore this familiar character in a new way? How could we tell the usual "Matlock defends an innocent man" story differently than they had done 110 times before?

Here is what we came up with:

Matlock is named a judge pro tem. Some other judge has a heart attack or something and Matlock has to sit in for him. He is presiding on a case where he can tell that the defendant is innocent, but the defense attorney is inept, and there is nothing he can do about it. He has to sit there and hear the evidence. The jury finds the man guilty of murder and Matlock has no choice but to sentence him to death. That is the first two acts. At the end of act two, Matlock goes and sees the guy on death row and says, "I'd like to help you." The poor innocent victim says, "Haven't you helped me enough? You are sending me to the electric chair." But Matlock smiles and says, "But you are innocent and now I am going to defend you on appeal." Now Matlock is defending a guy he has already sent up for murder.

The executive producer loved it. But we ended up getting involved in another series and *Matlock* was canceled in the interim. But we never forgot that pitch and use it as an example, as we have here, of how to do a character story that's different while still staying true to the franchise of the show, even one that has been on forever.

Oh, and by the way, when we pitched that idea, we had no idea what the crime in question was, or who had really done it, or how Matlock was going to prove this guy's innocence. We knew that if the executive producer liked the idea, we could work out these details later. We had the major story moves and the important conflicts for the lead—that's all that was important to the pitch.

Here's another example:

When we were hired as supervising producers on *Diagnosis Murder*, the show was essentially a clone of *Murder, She Wrote* and *Matlock*—an amiable whodunit with an established star playing a lovable professional who solves crimes on the side. That kind of series was a TV staple through the 1970s and 1980s, but by the time we got there, viewers had seen 100 *Matlocks*, 200 *Murder, She Wrotes*, a couple dozen *Father Dowlings*, and uncountable variations in between. We were having a hard time coming up with any kind of new twist that would keep us, let alone the audience, awake.

So we started thinking about the franchise. Dick Van Dyke wasn't a lawyer who solved crimes, or a mystery writer who solved crimes, or a priest who solved crimes. He was a *doctor* who solved crimes. That was something that none of the other shows had to play with. And yet very few of the crimes Dr. Mark Sloan solved had anything to do with medicine.

We decided to focus on Mark Sloan as a doctor, and to use his medical knowledge to solve his cases. We set one episode in the hospital during a emergency—a bus has crashed, and dozens of people are seriously hurt, with several dead. But Dr. Sloan soon realizes that one of the dead was actually murdered sometime between the accident and his arrival at the hospital. This realization and his discovery of the murderer are made possible only by his medical expertise. We got to see Dr. Sloan as a real doctor, and as a medical detective, for the first time.

We also did something else the show hadn't done before. We started crafting stories where whodunit took second or even third place behind how the mystery challenged who the characters were and their relationships with one another.

We devised an episode in which Dr. Travis, a young doctor, goes to visit Dr. Sloan, who lives on the beach. Dr. Travis is walking on the beach and sees a surfer collapse on the sand. Dr. Travis drags this guy to Dr. Sloan's beach house. Dr. Sloan tears open this guy's shirt and sees that this guy has smallpox. Despite their efforts, the man dies. But their troubles are just beginning.

Dr. Travis and Dr. Sloan are infected.

They are now quarantined in Dr. Sloan's house, dying of small-pox. They have to solve the murder of the surfer without even leaving their house, plus they have to stop this epidemic.

The story allowed us to deal with Dr. Sloan's sense of helplessness, and the quandary of trying to solve this crime while dying in his own living room. The story got us noticed at the network, and that episode, along with others like it, certainly played a significant role in our becoming the showrunners the following season.

As you begin thinking about ideas, ask yourself, "What can I bring to this show that no one else has been bright enough to bring to it yet?"

But be careful. Every series has questions that go unanswered—unaddressed, actually—for years, and it's not your job to change that.

For example, in the *Buffy* pilot we learned that Buffy is the latest in a long string of Slayers, and that when one dies, another will come to take her place. But until the fifth season, it never occurred to anyone to ask what had happened to the previous Slayers—why did they die, and is Buffy heading for the same fate? It would have been a great hook for a pitch, and a chance to explore another part of Buffy's character and situation. (They finally did that episode, but, like most good TV, it raised as many follow-up questions as it answered, leaving plenty of room for new stories.)

So don't tell the story that seems really obvious because odds are that not only have you thought of it, but every other freelancer has, too, and so have the producers. The long-lost wife returns. The alcoholic character falls off the wagon. The hero discovers a son he never knew he had. The hero's evil double shows up. The hero gets amnesia, goes blind, or is paralyzed.

If it's a science fiction show, it's the episode where everyone ages, or goes to the planet run by women, or is hurled into the past, or switches bodies with one another, or goes to the alternate dimension where they meet their mirror selves, to name just a few.

And you certainly don't want to tell the story that will change the course of the series. If it's a show built on the sexual tension between the two stars who haven't gone to bed yet, don't suggest the episode where they do. If it's a show about a guy looking for his lost son, don't pitch the story where he finds him. If it's a show about a guy on the run for a murder he didn't commit, don't have him clear himself of the crime.

Besides, none of those ideas is going to show the producer how clever, unique, and inspired you are.

Remember, you are not so much selling *ideas* as you are the *conflicts*. Two people heading toward one goal in different ways, getting in each other's faces, dealing with the obstacles thrown in their path. The conflict should make your characters reconsider who they are and how they confront situations, emotions, and problems. There should be a "character turn," showing growth or change in an individual, before the story ends. And the stories must be told in a four-act structure and stay within the boundaries of the show's franchise.

Once you've got all that down and you've come up with some interesting stories, you're ready to go in and pitch.

Fortunately, you've read this book, and you've done everything right. You go through a few days of worrying and wondering, calling your agent every two hours, and then you finally get the word.

You've got the assignment. Does this mean you can sit down and start writing the script?

Nope. Unfortunately, you still have a long way to go.

Exercises

- Watch a show and ask yourself what conflicts haven't been explored by the regular characters yet (being careful to stay within the franchise of the show, of course). Now ask yourself why the producers *haven't* explored these conflicts yet. Do this right, and by answering the question, you'll end up with some compelling story ideas.

- Watch your favorite show. Ask yourself what is the episode you wish they'd do, what would be the ultimate episode, and then ask yourself *why* they haven't done it yet. The answer could be the basis for a great spec episode, one that explores the core conflict of the series.

11

You've Got the Assignment, Now What?

If you pitch us a story and we like it, the next thing we have to do is pitch it to the network and the studio.

That's right, we have to pitch your pitch. We have to sell it the way you sold it to us (which is another good reason for the leave-behind). And once we get their approval and, inevitably, their notes, we can invite you in and start plotting the story together.

What? Isn't the story done yet?

Not even close.

What the producers have bought is your central conflict, maybe some supporting characters, the basic ideas. Now you're going to plot out the actual story—that is, you're going to figure out exactly which fifteen or twenty or twenty-five scenes are going to make up this episode.

The meeting could be just you and the executive producers, or it could include a few or perhaps all of the members of the writing staff. The process of "cracking the story" could take a day or more.

It usually begins with a general conversation about the story, different avenues the plot can take, and then, when a consensus is struck, the work moves to a large white board, where we start working with the beats, scene by scene, act by act, until a story emerges. It is this lively and arduous give-and-take that is the soul of television writing.

Each show, and each executive producer, has a different approach to plotting. For an example, check out the appendixes for an essay on how we plotted *Diagnosis Murder*. Maybe you like to start by sketching out the backgrounds of every character, but the producer likes to start by knowing what the finale will be and working backward. You'll do it his way, because it's his show. You need to adapt to his way of doing things, not the other way around.

Your job during the story meeting is to contribute plot moves and to honestly debate the pros and cons of ideas introduced in the room, but you always have to remember one thing: It's not your show. Ultimately, you are there to articulate the executive producer's vision, even if you think it's wrong. It's his show and his story, even if you did come up with the idea. Your responsibility as a freelancer is to give the producer the best episode you can according to the guidelines he sets out.

That doesn't mean the executive producer expects you to be an automaton, just sitting there agreeing with everything he says (well, most of us don't). You are expected to contribute. In fact, how you perform in the room while cracking the story is more important than your story idea and can even, ultimately, have a greater impact on your future than the script you will eventually write.

If you are good in the room, if you make valuable contributions to the development of the story and are fun to work with, then, even if you write a mediocre script, you might still earn more assignments and a staff job. Because the truth is, crafting stories is much harder than actually writing scripts. With a strong story in hand, a good producer can write a script (or rewrite a bad script) fairly quickly. It's working out the story that takes time and, frankly, is a more valuable skill to have on staff than being a terrific writer.

We never really understood this until we became producers. It used to make us crazy, for instance, that *Spenser: For Hire* kept hiring one particular writer for script after script—and every time, they would complain about how terrible the dialogue was. To our inexperienced eyes, it seemed crazy to keep hiring a writer who couldn't write.

It's true that this writer's scripts weren't great. What they were was easy to *rewrite*. You'd never want to shoot his original pages, but his stories and scenes were well structured. All the script needed was a dialogue pass, and for a producer who understood how the show's characters were supposed to sound, that was rarely more than a day's work. This freelancer had done all the hard work.

Some shows will actually send you off on your own to crack a story, but it's rare—and with good reason. There are practical matters about a show you can't know unless you are on staff. For example:

- The episodic budget.
- How many days must be spent shooting on interior sets as opposed to shooting on location.
- Which actors have contractual limitations that specify how many episodes per season they can appear in.
- That a particular actor will only work three days a week, no matter what.
- That a certain number of episodes must be produced within six days as opposed to the usual seven.

And that's only the beginning. The examples are endless, ever-changing, and unique to every show. But the executive producer knows it all and so does his staff. So if you come in with a story, they can shape it in a way that makes it fit with the creative and practical needs of the show.

The staff writers and story editors usually don't crack stories by themselves, either. They develop them with the entire staff, as a group, just like the freelancer does. It's done this way so everybody has a shared understanding of the story in case problems come up and one or more members of the staff are called in to help with story problems or rewrites down the line.

It especially helps when breaking stories with freelancers. That way, if the freelancer hits a problem spot while writing the story or the script and the executive producer happens to be in the editing room all day, he can call any member of the staff and they will be as familiar with the story as the executive producer is and give him a suggestion. Odds are, the suggestions made by one of the producers will be the same ones the executive producer would have given because their jobs are to second-guess and mimic him.

Before we were executive producers, half of our job was to come up with stories, and the other half was writing and telling those stories so that we sounded just like our boss. When we were doing *seaQuest 2032* our job as supervising producers was to come up with good stories told exactly the same way our executive producer, Patrick Hasburgh, would tell them.

We didn't write scenes as we would instinctively write them, the way that would reflect our abilities and our interests, but in the way that we knew Patrick Hasburgh would write the scene.

As a freelancer, that's your job, too.

But, again, we are getting ahead of ourselves. We were still in the story meeting. Let's get back to it.

Once everyone is clear on the plot moves, act breaks, and character arcs, the freelance writer is sent off to write the story, usually in the form of a **beat sheet,** a scene-by-scene description of what happens in an episode.

In a beat sheet, the entire episode is broken down into individual scenes and acts, usually six or seven scenes per act, four acts per episode. It's an outline, much like the one you might write before doing a big term paper. It's a list of the major dramatic and structural points of the story.

There are several examples of beat sheets in the appendixes, so we won't go into detail here. But if you flip ahead, what you'll see is that a beat sheet looks like a script without the dialogue. It has scene headings, like a script, but then it has just a paragraph explaining what happens in that scene.

We use the beat sheet to determine if there is really a script in your idea. Sometimes a great idea will fall apart once you actually try to mold it into a story.

A beat sheet does take some of the improvisation and inspiration out of writing the script, but the benefits far outweigh the negatives. Because the story is already worked out in detail, you can concentrate on the characters and the dialogue without worrying about the plot moves.

In a way, the process of television actually helps you turn out a better script because you are forced to think everything through before you finally sit down and churn out the teleplay. It also reassures the producer that the story works, and that you know where you're going as you write. And it provides an important production tool. While you're writing the script, the line producer (who is in charge of the physical production of the show) can use the beat sheet to start scouting locations, building sets, preparing a budget, and so forth.

So how long to do you have to write this all-important beat sheet? The Writers Guild of America says you have seven working days, but depending on the situation, we may ask you to turn it in faster than that—or tell you to take all the time you need.

No matter how long you have to write the beat sheet, take the assignment very seriously. Although it may be a relatively short document (anywhere from 6 to 20 pages, depending on the producer), it will determine your future on the show.

If we don't think from reading that beat sheet that you can do the script, we'll cut you off at story, rework that beat sheet, and hand it to another writer.

It's cruel, but that's the way TV works. Under WGA rules, an executive producer can let you go at several key points in the process and pay you for the work you've completed. It makes a lot of financial sense for them.

There is a lot of money riding on a screenplay. We aren't going to invest $27,000 in you unless we are convinced you can do the job.

There are some writers who will sell a lot of stories before actually writing a teleplay. Don't be offended by that. We may have confidence in your storytelling, but your scriptwriting skills may make us a little nervous.

There is a writer we know who makes a very good living in Hollywood but almost never writes a script. The thing is, he's a terrible writer, but his stories are really good. You'll see his credit frequently, story by him, screenplay by someone else. It frustrates the hell out of him, but at least he's working.

Don't let that anecdote worry you. He is the exception. Most of the time, we will buy the script from the same person we buy the story from.

Sometimes it helps to use dialogue in your beat sheet to show the conflicts in the scene. However, the risk is that we may think that the lousy sample dialogue in the beat sheet is your idea of *real* dialogue, and then we might get worried about your ability to write a useable script. So when we're freelancing, we usually don't use sample (or "temp") dialogue unless we are working with producers we know who trust us to write better dialogue for the actual script.

One of our pet peeves is getting a beat sheet that is full of bad temp dialogue that shows up in the script. It means the writer didn't even bother to think about the scene before he wrote it—he just took what was in the beat sheet and fleshed it out. We like to believe, and so do most producers, that when you are actually *writing* you are in a whole different frame of mind, so caught up in the characters that you are listening to their voices and not just copying the dialogue already written in your beat sheet.

Of course, there's a flip side to that, too. When you're working out stories, you generally throw out temp dialogue in the room. You know, "Renegade goes into the bar and says, 'If you think I'm going to back off, you're wrong, man' and then the bartender pulls out a gun." There have been times when an executive producer has spewed out such temp dialogue and then gotten furious when he discovered that it wasn't in the script. To him, these words tossed out in the room were precious as gold and needed to be preserved for the ages.

Once the beat sheet is turned in, we will give notes to the writer on the story before passing it on to the network and studio.

Or we might rewrite the story in-house and then submit it without involving the freelancer again. We do that for a couple of reasons.

The beat sheet isn't just a story, as you've probably gathered by now. It's also a sales pitch and a production document. It's used to get the network and the studio excited about the show. And it's used to begin the initial steps of production on the episode.

Once we get notes from the network, the studio, the line producer, the stars, and our palm readers, we put the writer "into script."

It's a formality for the producer, but so much more for you.

The moment you've worked so hard for has finally come. You're writing your first television episode.

Exercises

- Tape an episode of your favorite show. Now break it down into beats, scene by scene, act by act. Take this beat sheet and look at the four-act structure, the central conflicts, and the way stories play out. You're holding a snapshot of the series.
- Now take one of the story lines you came up with in one of our previous exercises and turn it into a beat sheet like the one you created in the last exercise.

12

Your First Assignment

You've written a script before, but that was on spec; this is the first time someone is actually *paying* you to do it.

That fact alone can be pretty daunting. In fact, it can be paralyzing.

When we wrote our first *Spenser: For Hire* on assignment, we spent the first day in terror. We couldn't get started. We couldn't stop thinking about how much we were being paid, and about how our futures in television, our dreams, were riding on this one script.

We immediately lost the ability to write.

Maybe we *never* knew how to write.

Maybe that first script was a fluke. An *unrepeatable* fluke.

We were ruined before we'd even started.

But the next day, rationality set in. We'd wasted our first day of work and we couldn't afford to waste another. We'd just have to pretend we weren't writing for money. This wasn't an assignment. We were writing for ourselves, for the pure pleasure of putting words down on paper, of creating characters, of spending hours playing make-believe.

And when we stopped thinking about everything that was riding on the script, when we concentrated on just the story and the characters, much of our stress disappeared, replaced by the agonies of wrestling a story off the outline and into action, character, and dialogue.

What we didn't know then was that at least for us, that first unproductive day would be a constant fact of writing life for us, even after hundreds of scripts to our credit. The old insecurities have simply been replaced by new ones: Will this script break our budget? Can it be shot in seven days? Will the story spark new clashes of egos between our cast members? Will we be able to finish it in time for production next Monday?

We've come to accept that our first day we'll either write nothing, or write crap. For some bizarre psychological reason, we just need that first day to settle in, to get into "writing mode," as we like to call it.

That's us. You may have your own insecurities, rituals, and methods of writing. It takes time to discover them and, more importantly, to make peace with them.

Once you get past your jitters and get into the work of writing, you will discover new problems. No matter how good the outline is or how thoroughly you thought you worked out all the story problems, you will encounter scenes that just don't play, motivations that don't feel real, and conflicts that feel contrived.

Your job is to solve those problems and stick as close to the spirit of the outline as possible. But if you find yourself deviating too far from the approved beats, or if the solution involves serious restructuring, call the producers first to get their okay.

Use your own good judgment. Producers are very busy, and they don't want to be called every time you encounter a bump while writing. If they wanted to wrestle with the everyday problems of writing a script, they would have written it themselves instead of hiring you.

As you write that first script for a series, it's wise to keep the sample screenplays you were given close by. You'll need to refer to those scripts for stylistic consistency and to remind yourself of the voices of the characters you're writing for.

Every show has its own stylistic rules as far as script format goes. For example, if you set a dialogue scene inside the hero's car, how do you refer to the location in the script? Is it:

INT. CAR – DAY

Or is it:

INT. MARK'S CAR – DAY

Or is it:

INT. THE MUSTANG – DAY

Or even, perhaps:

INT. MARK'S MUSTANG – DAY

How are the characters referred to in dialogue headings? Is it all by last name? All by first name?

For example, would it be:

> DR. SLOAN
> You might have pulled off the perfect murder—
> if only you hadn't sneezed.

Or would it be:

> MARK
> You might have pulled off the perfect murder—
> if only you hadn't sneezed.

Or is it:

> MARK SLOAN
> You might have pulled off the perfect murder—
> if only you hadn't sneezed.

These may seem like small details to you, but they aren't. And getting them wrong will not only irritate the producer, it will also make you seem lazy and inattentive. Before you start writing, it's a good idea to make a list of all the standing sets and locations and how they are referred to in the scripts. And be sure to double-check the spelling of all the characters' names and how they are dealt with in dialogue headings.

In a perfect world, your own insecurities and the inevitable story problems translating a story into a teleplay would be the only obstacles you'd encounter writing that first script. But television is far from a perfect world.

As we've said before, a series is a living thing that takes hundreds of people to make. The unexpected is expected on every episode. A storm hits the week you're shooting the episode that takes place at the beach—so it becomes a show that takes place in a warehouse. The star gets laryngitis two days into shooting an episode—so everything has to be rewritten to focus on the co-star instead. An episode focusing on the assassination of a senator has to be rewritten because two days before production begins a real senator gets murdered.

Nothing in film school or those weekend scriptwriting seminars prepares a writer for these kinds of creative obstacles, which occur far more often than you'd think.

Freelancers can get hit with them, too. It happened to us on our first professional assignment.

Remember that *Spenser: For Hire* we pitched and sold about the girl he witnesses jumping out of a window? It turned out the reason she jumped was that she was fleeing her lover and starting a new life, under a new identity, in Boston. But her lover tracked her down and to avoid being pulled back into a life with him, she tried to kill herself. Enter Spenser.

The twist Spenser discovers is that her lover also happened to be her brother.

It was definitely adult material, but that wasn't a problem. *Spenser* had already dealt with touchy subjects like abortion and was airing at the child-safe hour of 10:00 P.M. on a weeknight.

At least it was when we started writing.

We were midway through our script when ABC unexpectedly decided to move Spenser to 8:00 P.M. on Sundays between *The Wonderful World of Disney* and a new Dolly Parton variety show. Suddenly our brother–sister incest storyline was totally unacceptable for the time period.

So we got a call from the producers, who asked us to remove all references to incest, but to "keep everything else exactly the same" and to "maintain the integrity of the story."

In other words, they wanted us to keep the story, and all the scenes, exactly the same, but find a new motivation for everything the characters were doing. No big deal, right? Just substitute something else for incest.

Of course, it was a very big deal, and far from easy. Every scene, every encounter, was motivated by the backstory (as any good story should be). But we had no choice. Those were our orders.

We did what they asked. We kept the structure of the story exactly the same. We didn't deviate from the approved outline at all. The girl is still fleeing her brother, only now their shared secret isn't incest. She witnessed her brother murder their abusive father and, unable to deal with the horror and the guilt, she fled. Now her brother has found her and all the terrible memories have come flooding back. Unable to live with it, she tries to kill herself. Enter Spenser.

We weren't thrilled with the changes, but our customers—the producers and the network—were. We did the assignment and we handled the curveball they threw at us. They were so pleased, they immediately invited us to do another episode.

This wasn't the first, or the last, serious obstacle that would be thrown at us in the midst of writing a script, but we will always remember it because it was the experience that taught us just how unpredictable TV could be.

Many years later, when we were running the series *Martial Law*, we came up with an episode in which one of our characters, a detective played by Kelly Hu, went undercover as an arms dealer. To protect her, her mentor, a detective played by Sammo Hung, the star of the show (and a martial arts legend in China), went undercover as her butler. The story allowed us a great opportunity to explore, in a unique and entertaining way, the father–daughter and master–apprentice relationship between the two characters.

Sammo vehemently refused, for various creative and personal reasons, to play Kelly Hu's butler. Now, in a rational and reasonable world, Sammo would have objected when he got the outline, a full two weeks before the script was published. Or, since his objection was to the central concept of the episode, he might have said something when we put out our one-page proposal, which was sent to the stars at the same time it went to the network—before we started the long, arduous task of beating the story out.

But he didn't. And, frankly, we can't even claim that this was extraordinary behavior for a TV star. An actor generally focuses only on the show he's shooting, and doesn't really pay attention to what's coming up.

Since locations had already been set and guest stars hired, we couldn't throw out the script. So, a few days before production, we had to do a hurried rewrite while maintaining the inherent structure of the story.

In this new draft, we had Sammo go undercover as a butler to protect his partner, portrayed by Arsenio Hall, who was undercover as an arms dealer. While the story remained essentially the same, every single scene had to be rewritten to reflect the dynamics of this new situation. While we liked the previous draft, this new story had a lot going for it. We were able to have some great fun with their partnership and to explore their relationship from a whole new perspective. Imagine if Jackie Chan had to act as Chris Tucker's servant in a *Rush Hour* movie and you'll get the picture. You'll have to imagine it, because this draft of the script didn't get shot, either.

Sammo vehemently refused, for various creative and personal reasons, to play Arsenio Hall's butler.

It was now twenty-four hours before production was slated to begin . . . and once again we were doing another major rewrite. There was only one other regular cast member left, Gretchen Egolf, who played the young, relatively inexperienced leader of the Major Crimes Unit.

So we stayed up all night and rewrote the script again. This time, Gretchen went undercover as the arms dealer and Sammo was her butler. Same story, same structure, entirely different scenes.

You might ask why didn't we just have Sammo go undercover as the arms dealer and let one of our other cast members be the butler. We might have if it wasn't a dialogue-heavy part and Sammo, who spoke very little English, wasn't getting all his dialogue transmitted to him through a flesh-colored earpiece.

But the experience, although hellish at the time, actually taught us something (besides never to do a series with a difficult star who doesn't speak English). We learned it's possible to take the same basic story and recraft it in three entirely different ways.

We thought the experience would make for a great exercise in a screenwriting class some day. Little did we know it was preparation for a challenge we'd face a few years later.

One of the networks came to us and asked us to create a detective show around an eccentric, colorful, and outrageous professor of criminology. So we did. A few weeks after we turned in the pilot script, the network came back to us and said they loved it. They only wanted us to change one thing: the eccentric, colorful, outrageous professor of criminology.

Without changing the mystery or the structure of the story, could we just replace the central character with an entirely new one? How about a tough, streetwise, gritty professor of criminology instead?

It wasn't easy, but we did it.

At least we didn't have a crew waiting to shoot the pages the next morning.

The lesson of these anecdotes is that you have to be flexible, to be prepared to make major changes in the story even as you're writing it.

As a TV writer, you have to embrace changes because they will inevitably come. Your script will be rewritten, often for reasons that have nothing to do with whether or not you did a good job. You might get the chance to do the first rewrite; then again, you may just get paid off and all the revisions will be taken over immediately by the staff. Again, this is not necessarily a reflection on your ability or the quality of your writing. It's just the way it works.

Exercise

- In earlier exercises, we had you break down an episode of your favorite show into a beat sheet. Now take that beat sheet, pretend *you* wrote it, and prepare yourself for your rewrite notes. Here they are: We have to lose three exterior locations for budget reasons and have to find four more scenes to do on our regular standing sets (the interior locations used in every episode of the show, like the squad room in *NYPD Blue* or Tony Soprano's house in *The Sopranos*.) Now rewrite the beat sheet to address these notes, but without changing the plot of the story.

13

We've Got a Few Notes

Sometime after you turn in your first draft—it could be hours or weeks, depending on the show—you will get a call asking you to come back in for notes. Your writing fee includes a rewrite and a polish, and unless you've really screwed up (or the show has run out of scripts and needs a staff member to prepare yours for shooting next), the producers are going to get their money's worth out of you.

If you're really lucky, the phone call will contain a hint as to how your draft has been received. Odds are, though, it will be an assistant calling, and even though they usually know exactly what's going on, they'll never let on. If the assistant doesn't offer an opinion, don't ask. You'll find out soon enough.

So you're back at the writing offices, and after some obligatory chitchat, you'll get the verdict. "Nice work" or "Dynamite" means you've done well, and you're probably in for a pleasant notes session. "Really good first draft" could mean they liked it or hated it, but either way there are lots of notes coming. If you hear "Thanks for getting it done so fast," duck and cover—they think it's garbage.

But even if the producers aren't pleased with your first draft, don't panic. Your career isn't over yet. You've got a second chance to make them love you—and even better, they're going to tell you exactly how to do it.

When we started on *seaQuest 2032*, our first script was a disaster. We'd spent a lot of time with executive producer Patrick Hasburgh, listened to everything he had to say, then wrote a script the way we thought he wanted. He hated it. *Hated* it. **Hated** it.

Frankly, since we are human, our first inclination was to get defensive. (To say nothing of pouty.) *We did exactly what he asked for, this is what we've been talking about, doesn't he know this is what we should be doing. . . .* We spent an evening pissing and moaning to each other—that's one great thing about working with a partner—and got it all out of our system.

So the next morning, when we met with Patrick for a notes session everyone was clearly dreading, we were ready. Patrick started the session by trying to find something nice to say to us, but the look on his face made it clear what he was thinking: *I hired these guys as supervising producers, so I'm stuck with them, but how can I tell them I hate everything about their script without destroying them for the whole season?*

We didn't let him start. We said, "We know you hate the script. So forget it. Don't bother giving us notes on this draft, because we know it's all wrong." And we tossed our copy in the trash. "Now, let's go back to the outline and figure out how to make this a script you'll love."

With that, a cloud lifted. Patrick was visibly relieved, and we turned what could have been a brutal morning into a productive working session. We quickly came to understand what Patrick was looking for, and we turned out a new script that fit his vision of the show.

The only way we could do that was to take our egos out of the meeting. We had to remember that this script was not the poetic expression of our innermost hopes and dreams; it was to be an episode of *seaQuest 2032*. And the only person who could define what made a successful episode of *seaQuest 2032* was Patrick Hasburgh. Our first script might have been much worse or much better than our second (and since we haven't looked at either version in years, we can't even offer an opinion), but it really didn't matter. We weren't writing to please ourselves; we were writing to please the executive producer.

Somewhere in the world, there's probably a writer who enjoys getting notes. For most of us, it's among the least pleasant aspects of the job. Who wants to sit in a room and have their work torn apart, sometimes line by line?

But no matter how much you hate it, it's crucial that you stay calm, focused, and engaged during the session. What feels like criticism is actually a working process to turn your script from something the producers don't want into something they do. If you waste your energy getting defensive or feeling hurt, you will be incapable of contributing to the notes session.

The most important thing you can do when getting notes is to *listen*. That sounds obvious, but it's surprisingly difficult. When the executive producer is criticizing one of your choices, or even trashing your favorite thing in the entire script, your instinct is going to be to get defensive. To argue. To explain. To justify.

Don't.

For a producer, there's little more frustrating than trying to give a note and getting an argument back in return. Or an explanation. Honestly, we don't care that you meant the "walls of Jericho" scene as an homage to *It Happened One Night*—we think it's a cliché and we want you to change it. Say "got it" and move on.

But just agreeing with everything is rarely enough for a successful notes session. You have to listen to what's being said.

Sometimes, for instance, a producer will suggest a change you simply don't understand, or can't figure out how to work into the existing structure. If you're just writing down the notes, you might not notice that this note will create more problems than it can ever solve. At that point, it's not out of line to ask the reason for the note.

You see, people who give you notes are really trying to be helpful. Even the ones who are giving you notes that will destroy everything you've worked to achieve in your script are trying to be helpful. And part of that helpfulness sometimes comes in the form of solutions to problems they've encountered.

Of course, there are solutions that cause more problems than they solve. In that case, it can be useful to ask what problem the note is trying to fix—once you understand what the trouble is, you might have another solution.

Generally, you're going to get two kinds of notes. First come the *overall* notes. These are probably the most serious—questions about tone, style, characterization, and structure will fall into this category.

One tiny overall note can end up changing everything in your script—*You know, I just can't believe that after seeing Oz, Dorothy would want to go back to Kansas.* Now there might be an easy fix for that problem—*It's not Kansas she cares about; it's Auntie Em.* But it might lead to your entire story being dismantled—*Okay, she's not going to see the wizard, she's looking for affordable housing in a Munchkin-free neighborhood and . . .*

Overall notes come in two varieties. The first isn't too bad: *Here's what we don't like, and here's how to fix it.* As long as you can make sense of what you're being told, you've got a road map to follow for your rewrite. It's the other kind that's the killer: *Here's what we don't like; fix it.* What that means is, we've got a problem with no solution, find one.

When you find yourself with a note like that, don't just write it down and move on. This is one time where discussion is important. You need to understand what they don't like about the current version; you can't fix it if you don't understand what's not working. Try floating a suggestion in the room. Even if it's not the right solution, it should spark a discussion that might solve the problem. If there's a serious story problem, it's in no one's best interest to let you leave the room without an idea for a fix.

After the overall notes, the producers will give you *line* or *page* notes: Change this line, our character would never say that, this joke isn't funny, this scene is half a page too long, cut this, add that. There could be a handful of these notes, or a hundred. Sometimes a producer will hand you his copy of the script with his line notes in it—take it gratefully and make sure you do everything he's put in there. Don't get cute and say, "Well, I did these ten notes, so I don't have to do those five." If a line bothers a producer enough to give you a note on the first draft, it's going to bother him even more if he sees it again.

By the way, this sounds so incredibly obvious that we're tempted not to mention it, except that we've been burned this way a couple of times: When someone is giving you notes, *write them down.* It's infuriating for a producer, who has probably put in hours of thought on how to redo your script, to give notes to a writer who nods, smiles, and doesn't write down a word.

Granted, it's possible that you have such a good memory that you don't need even to jot down a word or two. But several writers have told us about their amazing memories, and their rewrites rarely included any of the notes they were given. You can't imagine how angry this makes producers—we're taking valuable hours out of our day for this session, and if you ignore our notes, we've wasted time we'll never get back.

So even if you do have a perfect memory, write down the notes. It will make everyone in the room happier.

It's a good bet that you're going to come out of your first notes session exhausted. You'll feel as if you've been physically assaulted. And you'll probably wonder how you'll ever be able to accomplish everything you've been told to do in the week or so you've been given.

Don't panic yet. We've had notes sessions that went on for hours and seemed to demand an entire rewrite, but when we got home and actually went through the notes, we discovered there was really only a half a day's work. On occasion we've done rewrites in less time than it took to get the notes.

On the other hand, we've also had some very short and easy notes sessions, and then have gone home to discover that the two small overalls we got meant an entire restructuring of acts two through four.

Sometimes you'll get notes you absolutely hate. That destroy your script. That pervert everything you'd ever hoped to accomplish as a writer. What do you do then?

Simple: Do the notes.

And do them well.

We know what you're thinking—*I'm a writer, not a whore. I have to maintain my integrity.*

We're not going to address the issue of integrity—we're TV writers. But we can give you one reason why you should do the notes, do them to the best of your ability, and do them with a smile:

Whether you do it or not, the note is going to get done.

A television show isn't a democracy; your opinion doesn't have as much weight as the executive producer's. And if he wants the script to go a certain way, you can be sure that when you see the show on the air, that's the way it's going to go.

Remember that first *Spenser: For Hire* we pitched and sold? Lose the incest but maintain the integrity of the story?

How do you think we felt when we got that note?

Sure, we sound calm and mature now when we talk about it. At the time, what we felt was rage. Black, desperate rage. How could they butcher our story this way, especially since it was a story everybody liked? If we got a note like that today, we'd sigh, shrug, and get to work. But we were young and inexperienced then, and we argued. And argued.

Fortunately Bill Yates and co-executive producer Steve Hattman were extremely patient with new writers. They understood how we felt, and they took the time to let us vent. But they also understood what the network needed. And by the end of the conversation, so did we. We realized that someone was going to change our script to take the incest out—and that we would probably be happier with the result if we were the ones to do it.

There's no denying the script that was shot wasn't nearly as strong as our original draft. But no one was ever going to shoot our original draft. Refusing to do the notes would not have been protecting what we'd written, it would merely have caused trouble for the very kind and generous producers who would have had to do the rewrite themselves.

After you turn in your second draft, you may or may not be called back in to do a polish. This should be a much smaller set of notes—line tweaks, location changes, and so on. You probably won't be asked to do substantial work at this point. If the producers still have major problems with your script, they'll do the next draft themselves.

(One small hint: *Always* keep all your drafts. You never know when someone is going to say, "You know, I liked the line in the last draft better," and if that happens, you really need to be able to find out what that line was and put it back in.)

And that's it. Your work is finished, your script is done.

Except that from now until production, colored pages will start turning up in your mailbox. Each time a revision is made to a script, the changes are printed on a colored and dated page. This way, the production team can easily keep track of when a revision was made, and what the most recent revision is. The colored pages are printed in a specific order (pink, then blue, then green, etc.), so that even if you don't look at the date at the top of the page, you'll know which revisions are the most recent. And each individual change on the colored page is also marked with an asterisk, so you can immediately spot which scene, location, or dialogue has been reworked. By the time an episode is done, a typical script will be a multi-colored collection of pages reflecting all the revisions that have been made during the course of the production.

What this constant stream of pages coming into your mailbox means is that someone, somewhere, is still giving notes. Those notes may be minor changes, like changing a location or a word of dialogue, or an entire rewrite of a page, an act, or even the whole script.

No matter how many people have commented on your script, there's always another set of notes coming down the line. First it's the producers. Then the studio. Then the network. Then, once it's approved, it's production. And then it goes to the actors.

The good news for you is that as a freelancer, you're going to be protected from most of this. Under the WGA contract, all you're required to deliver is a story, first draft, second draft, and a polish.

The bad news is that your script is not protected.

In one way or another, those notes are going to affect your script.

Producers are bombarded with notes on the script from dozens of different sources. Beyond the network and studio notes, there are the comments from the actors, the director, the line producer, the stunt people, the location scout, the wardrobe department, and the rest of the department heads. Not all the notes are creative; many are practical and involve changes necessary to make the show on budget and within the shooting schedule. And some are just nuts.

We've received lots of helpful, insightful, and creative notes that have immeasurably improved our scripts. Of course, the ones we remember are the bad ones.

Some of the most bizarre notes come from Broadcast Standards, the network censors who are charged with making sure no one ever gets offended by a television program. But sometimes they find offense in the strangest places.

In one script, for the short-lived George Segal detective series *Murphy's Law*, we had a woman lamenting about her dirty bathroom, complaining that "the fungus grows back faster than I can scrape it off." The network censor asked us to "remove the sexual reference." We're still trying to figure that one out.

In another episode of *Murphy's Law*, our characters went to the zoo, and the network censor warned us "not to show any sequences of monkeys copulating." That, of course, dashed our plans for an exciting finale.

We were also advised not to have one character refer to another as a "moron" because we would "offend all the morons in the audience." They urged us to replace "moron" with "idiot" or "yutz." We declined to make the change, explaining that all the morons in the audience were watching our competition.

Even when the script is finally in production, it still isn't safe. Now come the actors. Sometimes they'll actually read the script ahead of time and alert the producers if they find a problem. But generally, TV actors focus exclusively on the script that's being shot. And when they do demand changes, it's far too late to do it in a reasoned, thoughtful manner. When a star won't come out of his dressing room until the script is changed, and there's a crew standing around costing $100,000 every hour, work or no work, the first solution ends up being the best solution.

One actor we worked with would routinely cross out entire pages of dialogue, informing us that he would "say it all with a look." It wasn't because he had an emotive face. No matter what the situation—lust, anger, fear or pain—we got the same stony look. He did it because he couldn't remember his lines. Even "hello" was reduced to a nod of the head.

Not one of these notes we've just shared with you had anything to do with the quality of the writing—but they had everything to do with the collaborative reality of making a TV show. Everyone wants, and gets, some input. Some of that input is valid, some of it isn't.

The bottom line, though, is that the script that gets shot will often end up being very different than the one you turned in. If you're smart, you won't complain. You'll accept it as the standard operating procedure in television and start working on your next pitch. You'll accept it because you know that if you work hard enough as a freelancer, eventually you'll get hired on staff and work your way up to producer, where you will be able to control your work and ultimately decide what gets changed and what doesn't.

Exercise

- Give your story ideas to your significant other, best friend, or worst enemy and ask for an opinion. Try to listen without arguing, getting defensive, or being nasty—and remember to write down all their notes. Remain cordial and thank them for their comments. Wait a day and come back and look at the notes. Now that you've had a chance to calm down, you might be surprised by how many of the notes actually improve the story, or change it in a way that doesn't really do any harm. You can do something now you can rarely do in TV— incorporate the notes that work for you and discard all the others.

14

Am I There Yet?

All the hard work is finally over. You've done it. You've finished your first freelance script assignment for a TV series.

You've cashed the checks (and who knew they took out so much in taxes?). You've got your Writers Guild card (and who knew they were going to charge so much for your initiation fee?). You've called everyone you've ever met to tell them when your episode is going to be on (and who knew how many of your friends were going to ask to borrow money?).

You've made it. You're a professional TV writer now. After all the years of struggling, after all the impossible obstacles thrown in your path, you've succeeded. You're not a wannabe any more.

Feels good, doesn't it?

In fact, now would be a good time to visit the BMW dealership and take a couple test drives before you get inundated with script assignments.

And you know you will be. You're an industry insider now. It's the first sale that's hard, the rest come easy.

You'd think so, wouldn't you?

Well, don't quit your day job just yet.

It's going to be very tempting, because unless you're making a career switch from lawyer or doctor, you've probably just about doubled your annual gross income with this one script sale. You can afford to quit Kinko's or Starbucks or Merry Maids or wherever you're working to pay the bills. One more script sale and you might even be able to ditch the roommate or the parents and move into your own place.

There's only one small problem: There's no guarantee that the second sale is going to be any easier than the first. Unless the showrunner who bought your first script is already asking you for a second, you're essentially starting from zero all over again.

Hardly seems fair, does it?

Welcome to the television business.

From the outside, the TV business can look like one big club. You see the same names popping up on show after show. It's pretty clear that once you're in, you're in. And you're definitely on the right side of that door now.

Unfortunately, that's not how it works. Even long-established writers have to fight for every job they get. Writers with big credits often have big mortgages, too. And we all want to keep working.

But you're not really competing with those guys, right? They're after jobs as supervising producers and co-executive producers, and all you want is a mere freelance script assignment.

In fact, you *are* competing with those guys. But we'll get to that shortly.

We were lucky when we started. After our first sale to *Spenser: For Hire*, the producers bought three more scripts from us. Then one of the producers recommended us to his friend, producer Glen Larson, who was looking for freelancers for one of his new shows. And then we were off and running, working pretty much nonstop for years.

That's a best-case scenario. (Or an almost-best-case scenario anyway. We didn't get our own show on the air, a $10 million development deal, or an Emmy right away. In fact, we're still waiting.)

A more typical experience happened to our friend Barney. He toiled for years as a producer's assistant, typing their scripts, answering their phones, making their appointments. And, like so many assistants, he was spending all his free time writing specs, hoping for a career as a writer.

Finally, after years of struggling, it happened for him. Barney sold a pitch to *The Outer Limits*. He wrote the script, the episode was shot, and he was thousands of dollars richer.

Barney immediately quit his job and, vowing never to type any-one else's script ever again, devoted himself to the life of the profes-sional writer.

He didn't get another job for two years.

Two years.

Sure, he got meetings. He studied shows, prepared pitches, did everything the right way . . . and nothing clicked. After nearly a year of unemployment, he was forced to go back to being an assistant again, and all the money he'd made from the first script was gone.

Barney was working as a script coordinator when he made his next sale, only this time, he kept his day job and stuck the writing money in the bank as an emergency fund. Frustrating as it was, he kept working at his paying, non-writing job while looking for the next script.

The good news is, more assignments did come, and he eventu-ally landed on the writing staff of a syndicated adventure series. Only then, with the security of a weekly paycheck, did he give up his day job as a script coordinator.

When you make that first sale, celebrate. But assume there isn't going to be another sale for a long time. And then start working to prove yourself wrong.

How do you do that? By doing exactly what you were doing *before* you became a big-shot TV writer. That means you've got to keep flipping burgers, bagging groceries, cleaning pools, or whatever else you were doing to pay the bills. And you've got to start writing another spec script.

You thought you were beyond that now, didn't you? You've already got a spec script. A damn good one. Good enough to get you work. And you've got the script you wrote for the TV show. That should be enough. Why write another script for free now that you're a pro?

For one thing, it will keep you busy, sharpen your skills, and help keep you from thinking about where your next job will come from.

But beyond the psychological distraction, there are a couple of practical reasons for writing another spec. If your agent is any good, a lot of people have already read your first spec, not only the producers who hired you, but all of those who didn't. They're not going to reconsider hiring you just because that same spec hits their desk again.

What about that script you just got paid for? Why can't your agent send that all over town instead of a new spec?

If your first assignment is on *Law & Order, CSI, NYPD Blue,* or another prestige show, he can. But the odds are that your first assignment won't be for one of those shows. Those series have huge writing staffs who do almost every episode. And while it's true that WGA rules mandate a certain number of freelance assignments—or, at least, meetings—per season for every show on the air, that's not going to help you much.

When *ER* commissions a script from a freelance writer, they want someone who will make the process of generating an episode easier, not harder, than doing it in-house. Especially because this means a staff member is giving up a script fee. They want someone who they know will deliver.

The good news for them, and the bad news for you, is that every member of that large staff knows at least two good, experienced writers who'd love a shot at the show. There are at least a dozen people standing in front of you for that job. And many of them are going to be those established writer-producers we were talking about before, the ones you wouldn't think would care about a simple freelance assignment.

So that's why your first script probably won't be a show like *The Practice* and probably will be something like *Mutant X* or *Witchblade* or *Andromeda,* shows with small staffs and limited budgets. Which means, probably, first-run syndication or basic cable.

Hey, we're not putting down low-budget TV. We had a great time doing *She-Wolf of London* and *Cobra* for first-run syndication (What do you mean you've never heard of those shows? They're classics!), but assignments on those shows don't impress network showrunners. We know it from personal experience on both sides of the desk.

Breaking into television isn't easy. *Staying* in is even harder.

We aren't saying you won't get another assignment, we're just saying it's going to take a lot of work, patience, and perseverance, which you obviously have, or you never would have made that first sale.

Now that you're a professional TV writer, it's not enough to just write another spec and pray for the next job to come along. You've got to take care of business, too.

While you're writing that spec, keep watching television, especially the new shows, because that's where you have the best chance of making a sale.

Stay in touch with your friends from those screenwriting classes we told you to take. Odds are a few of them are becoming professional TV writers, too, and beyond providing emotional support, they could have some good leads for you.

Try to keep in contact, without becoming a nuisance or a stalker, with the producers you sold that first script to. They are in the best position to get you work, if not on their show, on a series run by one of their friends.

Make a habit of taping the pilot episode of each new series, and maybe an episode or two after that, so you have them on hand in case a pitch meeting comes up. Or, better yet, think up a couple of story ideas for each show, call your agent, and ask him if he can get you a meeting with the showrunner to talk about them.

You need to know who the players are if you want to become one yourself, so pay close attention to the credits of every show you watch, new or old. Make it a priority to know who the successful writers and producers are, what they are working on now, and what they did in the past.

And it doesn't hurt to keep an eye on the competition, the other freelance writers like yourself, what they are writing and who they are writing for. Once you recognize the names, you'll be able to see for yourself which shows use more freelancers than others and where you might have the best shot at getting in.

Read *Daily Variety* and *The Hollywood Reporter* to keep yourself informed about which shows are in development, which are being ordered, and how the new shows on the air are performing. There's no point coming up with a half-dozen great story ideas for a show that's going to be canceled after the third episode.

A lot of this, of course, is your agent's job. While it's his job to find work for you, it helps if you're informed about the industry and can point him to shows or producers you think might be good opportunities for you.

Your agent needs to sell you to producers, and you can help him do that. You need to give your agent a sense of what kind of shows you like to watch, what kind of shows you think you could write for, and what types of shows to avoid. You don't want your agent putting you up for every show; you want him putting you up for the *right* ones.

We've always enjoyed watching and writing mysteries, cop shows, and action-adventure stuff, so that's what we had our agent put us up for. We knew we weren't the right guys for shows like *Seventh Heaven, Touched by An Angel,* or *Once and Again* because, for one thing, they are shows we'd never watch. We wouldn't have a clue how to write for them. So we have our agent focus his attention where our talents and our interests are, which is why you won't see a single spiritually uplifting, emotional family drama among our credits.

Now that you've made that first sale, the good news is you'll have an easier time getting pitch meetings. Once you do line up your first pitch as a professional writer, it's going to be your first experience all over again. At least you've been through it before, and since you know you can do the job, you're bound to be more confident. That's good. But don't be cocky. Go into each meeting as if it's your first, and don't get bitter if you don't make a sale. You're gaining valuable experience and making good contacts for the future.

When you go in for pitches, keep in mind that you aren't just looking to make a sale, you're also selling yourself and your professionalism. You may not get an assignment that day, but if you impress the producer, he'll invite you back again. Or he might remember you if an opening comes up later on. Or he might recommend you to other showrunners he knows (and you can bet he knows a lot of them).

When we were freelancers, we pitched *Beauty and the Beast* repeatedly and couldn't make a sale. In fact, one of the pitches went so badly that we were convinced they hated us and would never invite us back. Then one day we got a call. They had a freelance script that needed a complete rewrite, would we be interested in doing it?

We did the rewrite for them, and although we turned out to be the first in a long line of writers who'd take a crack at that script, it was a paying gig, one we got by making a good impression over several pitch meetings.

Eventually, one freelance assignment will lead to another. And if you're good at what you do, you won't stay a freelancer very long. You'll end up on the staff of a TV series.

It can happen in one of two ways.

The most common way is simply to do a terrific job for a producer. When a freelancer writes a great script, works well in the room, and really gets the show, you can bet the showrunner will quickly give him a multiple-episode deal or grab him on staff fast before someone else does. Good, dependable writers aren't easy to find, and when a showrunner finds them, he keeps them.

The other way is to build up a reputation with a body of work, writing solid, dependable scripts for a wide range of shows. It will only be a matter of time, if you haven't been snatched up yet, before network and studio development executives will begin to notice your name and your work. When staffing season comes up, you'll be among the writers that development executives recommend to producers for the entry-level staff writer and story editor positions.

And when that happens, you can quit flipping burgers. You won't be a professional TV writer anymore. You'll be a professional TV writer who just might be making a living at it.

Just don't throw out the apron and spatula—at least not until you're at your Malibu beach house living comfortably on your residuals.

Ah yes, residuals—one of the best things about writing for television.

Every time a show is rerun, either on the network or in syndication, or rebroadcast overseas, you get a royalty payment, also known as a **residual.** The amount of that residual is based on all sorts of arcane and complex formulas we won't get into here, but the bottom line is, it's money. And it's money that will show up unexpectedly in your mailbox for years, as long as the episode you wrote is still being shown somewhere. If you write enough episodes, those residual checks will become an important part of your income and can even sustain you between assignments.

But the holy grail of TV writers isn't the next freelance assignment, or finding a fat residual check in the mailbox. It's getting on the writing staff of a TV series.

Exercise

- Go through all the exercises you've done so far . . . and do them over. No, we aren't joking. Just because you've done this once doesn't mean you've mastered it. You're going to have to keep repeating the same experience over and over as you work your way up in television. So write up another beat sheet based on another episode of a show you like. Now repeat the frustrating and difficult notes we gave you before.

15

Becoming Rob Petrie

Television writing jobs come with dozens of titles: story editor, producer, consultant, senior supervising producer, executive consultant, senior executive supervising consultant. But there are really only two jobs for writers: freelance and staff.

Staff is the one you want.

Many years ago, a writer could make a good living as a freelancer. In the 1950s and 1960s, most dramas would produce up to thirty-nine episodes a year with only one writer on staff and multiple script assignments handed out to freelance writers.

But by the time we got into the business in the late 1980s, those days were gone for good. All shows now had at least a handful of writers on staff, and they generated most of the scripts themselves.

There are some older writers who resent the way the business changed. But there are two great advantages to the staff system: money and control.

Let's look at the money first. As a freelancer, you get a nice check for writing a script—something around $27,000 for a network show, a little more than half that for cable or syndication—and you get more checks when your show reruns. Not bad, until you see what you're missing.

Once you're on staff at story editor level or above, you get a weekly paycheck of several thousand dollars. Salaries vary greatly, but WGA *minimum* for a story editor position is somewhere close to $5,000 per week. And on top of that, you still get paid the same $27,000 or so for your scripts.

The money is great, there's no denying. But in some ways, the control you get from being on staff is even more important. As a free-lancer, you bang out your two drafts and a polish, put the script outside your front door for the messenger to pick up, and a couple months later you turn on the TV and see something that may or may not resemble what you wrote.

When you're on staff, there's still a good chance your script is going to be rewritten. But you're going to be there for the entire process. You're going to participate in the evolution of your script. You'll help the director prep, you'll have a voice in casting the guest parts, you'll observe the shooting on set, you may even have a chance to consult on the editing. You're not just writing scripts anymore; you're making television.

And—did we mention this part?—you're getting paid a ton of money for doing it.

It sounds wonderful, doesn't it? Well, it is. But, yes, there is a catch. People who pay you this much money for doing a job feel free to make fairly extravagant demands on your time. You may find yourself working seven days a week for months at a time, getting phone calls demanding a script at two o'clock on a Saturday morning, or just being at the constant beck and call of your executive producer.

The fact is, when you join a writing staff, you are signing away your entire life to the showrunner. In a business that rewards only success and punishes only failure, there are almost no checks on what an executive producer can ask of you.

We once worked for a tremendously successful producer who was famous for shanghaiing his writing staff. You'd come into work one day, and he'd decide the entire staff should work at his house. His Palm Springs house. Or he'd ask a writer to conduct a notes meeting in his limo, which would take them to the airport . . . where he'd continue the meeting on his private jet . . . which would take them to the producer's Hawaii house, where the writer would have to stay until the script was done.

We never had the opportunity to get kidnapped this way, because we alienated this producer early in our relationship with him. We'd turned in our first draft on a Monday, and he called that

Wednesday to schedule a notes session at his house for the following day. We asked to postpone the meeting, as we were both going to be out of town that Thursday—it was Thanksgiving. He never forgave us.

Other showrunners like to play power games with their staffs. We've heard lots of stories from female writers about male executive producers who like to make speakerphone calls to sex services in the middle of notes sessions, or schedule mandatory staff meetings at strip clubs. Sure, the women could probably make a good case for sexual harassment, but in a business where everyone knows everyone, few people are going to risk their careers over such a lawsuit.

And God forbid you ever get a showrunner who's going through a divorce and can't stand the thought of going home. Trust us, you will be there to share the pain, every night. And unlike the divorce lawyers and shrinks, you don't get to charge by the hour.

Essentially, your experience on a writing staff will depend on the personality of the showrunner. We were unbelievably lucky on our first staff job, on the short-lived comedy-mystery *Murphy's Law*. We worked for a gentleman named Michael Gleason, who was (and still is) patient, brilliant, kind, and generous. He saw that we were ambitious and energetic, and he allowed us as staff writers access to aspects of production that some of our friends never got when they were supervising producers.

But the greatest lesson that Michael taught us was that making TV shows should be *fun*. Sure, there are miserable days, and hard battles, and inevitable disappointments. But we're all doing exactly what we want to do, and we should enjoy it.

That lesson has kept us sane during our entire career. But it has also caused a few problems. Having internalized Michael's viewpoint from our first staff job, it's left us with little patience for the showrunner who believes that if you're not miserable, you must not be doing your job right. And there are plenty of those.

In fact, right after *Murphy's Law* was canceled, we went to work for Michael's polar opposite. This guy—oh, let's just call him Ferd— was a very talented writer on his first showrunning gig. There was just one trouble:

He could never make up his mind.

You have to understand, there's really only one skill an executive producer needs to succeed: he has to be able to make a decision and communicate it. That's it. If his decisions are good, the show's a hit; if they're bad, the show's a flop. But either way, until he makes up his mind, no one else can do their job. Stories and scripts can't get written, actors can't be cast, locations can't be scouted. And every delay ends up costing money. Lots and lots of money.

So there we sat, day after day, in an airless, smoke-filled room, while Ferd dithered. (Did we mention that Ferd was a chain smoker? Even back then it was probably illegal to force your employees to inhale your smoke all day—it definitely is today in California—but as a story editor what are you going to do? Report him to OSHA? Right.) It wasn't that Ferd couldn't come up with story ideas, it was that he couldn't stop. He'd have a brainstorm in the morning— *There's a serial killer out there, and he's killing nuns!*—and the staff would spend a few days locked in the smoke pit working out the beats of the story, until it was finally just about done.

And then Ferd would come in the next morning and say he'd had a new brainstorm—*We got it backward, guys. There's a nun out there . . . and she's killing serial killers!* And we'd erase off the whiteboard the four acts worth of beats and get to work on the new idea until it was almost done, and we got thrown for a new twist—nuns and serial killers teaming up to kill cops, or something.

In retrospect, we can see that Ferd must have been terrified. This was his first showrunning gig, and he desperately wanted it to go well. But to two neophyte story editors, he just looked like a nut.

And as the weeks ticked by and not a single story came out of his office, he began to panic. He would call us into his office on a Friday and order us to work over the weekend—but until he cleared a story, there was no work we could do. He'd scream at us for coming in as late as 8:30 A.M. (most TV staffs get to work between 9:30 and 10:00), even though he was always tied up in meetings until long after 10:00 A.M. and had forbidden the staff to do any story work while he was out of the office. And the one time the rest of the staff took advantage of his absence and beat out an entire story (in one afternoon!), he flew into a rage and erased the entire board without even reading it when he saw what we had done.

It was a month before production was going to start, and already the office was unbearable. Our stomachs were manufacturing more acid than Monsanto, we had blinding headaches half the day, and we were developing bad cases of smoker's cough. And because we had started out working for Michael Gleason, we knew the truth: *It didn't have to be this way.*

Finally, we'd had enough. The end came when Ferd found out one of us had hosted an out-of-town guest over the weekend . . . *without clearing it with him first.* It was an outrageous demand, made even more so by the sad fact that we couldn't have worked over the weekend if we'd wanted to, since Ferd had still not cleared a story.

That was the one job we ever quit. We walked out on a hit show and went to work on a series that looked like career suicide—*Baywatch.* But the executive producer of *Baywatch* was Ernie Wallengren, who'd been the supervising producer on *Murphy's Law,* and we knew that no matter how bad the show might turn out to be, the work experience would be good. And it was. Despite the enormous creative difficulties *Baywatch* presented, and the often soul-sapping quality of the writing we were doing, we woke up every morning looking forward to getting to work.

And Ferd, not surprisingly, didn't make it through the year as executive producer. He just didn't have the skills it took to run a show.

So what was he doing there? Well, there's the funny thing about showrunning. You rise to the level of executive producer because you're a good writer, but when you get there, you find out that 80 percent of the job is management. And the skills it takes to be a good writer have nothing to do with what it takes to be a good manager.

Ferd made lots of mistakes in his short tenure. And one of the first, probably, was hiring us. Oh, we didn't think so at the time. But he hired a team of story editors who had an entirely different philosophy of what life on a staff should be like. He needed writers who would be scared of him, who would do whatever he said and never question why. But he didn't know that: he thought he wanted independent thinkers, and he got us.

Casting a writing room is a delicate process and is just as important as casting your actors. We know what we need to see in writers, for instance. Beyond the initial talent, we want tough, confident people who will fight for their ideas in the room, and who won't be afraid to challenge us. Maybe it's because we're partners and we're used to arguing over ideas with each other, but we want our staff to feel they can express their honest emotions about any story idea or scripted scene. And we need them to be hard enough that we can shoot down ten of their ideas in a row and they still come back with number eleven.

That's so natural to us, it's always a surprise that anyone wants anything else. There was one writer we interviewed who'd been a story editor on a hit show. We read the scripts he'd done for the show, and they were great—and were essentially what had been filmed. But his contract hadn't been renewed, which of course made us wonder why. His agent explained: the hit show's executive producer felt he was "too enthusiastic." That EP liked a quiet room, where he could think out loud and the staff would take notes.

We scoffed at such a silly idea for firing a writer. Who cares about personalities if you can write? And then we interviewed a young woman for the same job. She had written a great script, and the meeting was really just a formality. But the second she walked in the room, we knew it would never work out. She was pleasant, polite, clever—and shy. Even in the interview, her voice never rose above a whisper, and her eyes stared down at the table most of the time. And we knew, as much as we liked her writing, that she would never last on our staff. She just wasn't tough enough. (Fortunately, another show snapped her up a week later.)

Over the years since the Ferd fiasco, we've worked for lots of showrunners, some of whom have become good friends, some of whom should have been tried for war crimes. But we managed to have decent relationships with all of them, because we have a simple philosophy of working on staff:

It's your show. Tell us what you want, and we will give it to you.

And we mean that. We will, of course, present our point of view, but once the showrunner has made up his mind, we're going to do our best to fulfill his vision. That's why we're there.

If you want to succeed in television, you will do the same thing. And if you want to *survive* in television, there's something else you have to do. What you have to do is simple, it's obvious, and it's almost impossible to pull off:

Save your money.

When you're working, money is going to start flooding in. It's probably more money than you've ever seen before. And after a couple years of steady work, you're going to feel like it's never going to stop.

It will.

Just about every writing career has huge ups and downs. You may work steadily for a decade and then not be able to get a freelance gig for three years. Why? Who knows? It happens.

And as long as you're aware it's going to happen, you can be okay. Live a nice life, take fabulous vacations, drive a German car, buy a mansion . . . but whatever you do, make sure you sock some of that money away. Don't live a lifestyle that requires constant huge infusions of cash—clerks at Wal-Mart live from paycheck to paycheck because they don't have a choice. You do. Make the right one.

And remember, when you're working your ninth straight week without a break, when you're rewritten the same script thirty-seven times, when you jump in fright every time the phone rings . . . it's just a TV show.

Exercise

- We wish there was an exercise we could give you to prepare you for the experiences of being on the staff of a television series and for managing the sudden changes in your life. All we can really ask you to do is read this chapter over again and remember the advice we passed on to you, advice that was passed on to us from experienced producers. The advice saved us a lot of heartache . . . and our houses.

16

Rewrites

So you're reading that last chapter, and one question keeps coming to mind:

I'm on staff and I'm working twenty-four hours a day. . . . What the hell am I doing all that time?

Believe it or not, most of it, you're writing.

Actually, you're rewriting.

Granted, you'll probably be spending a lot of time in the writing room, helping to crack stories. But much of the rest of your days will be spent in front of the computer.

Remember back when you were a freelancer, and you kept getting colored script pages in your mailbox every day?

Congratulations. Now you're the one putting those pages out.

As we've said repeatedly, TV is a business. Every show has a budget and a schedule, and every script has to fit both of those demands.

And what you have to understand is that everything you put in a script takes time and costs money. *Everything*.

Let's say you type this simple line:

EXT. STREET – DAY
A CAT ambles off the sidewalk and is run over by a car.

Congratulations, you've just spent tens of thousands of dollars.

But how? First of all, there's the cat. Granted, you can often get a kitten for free. But you need one that will do what you want when you want, because the last thing you can afford is to have your entire crew sitting around waiting for an untrained animal to go in the right direction. So you need a show-biz cat. And of course, that cat comes with a show-biz trainer who is going to get paid.

Then there's the car. Is that one of your regulars driving that car? If not, you probably can't use one of the few picture cars the show owns, since they're identified with the characters who drive them, and you'll have to rent one. Of course, you need a driver. And not just any driver, a stunt driver who—surprise!—gets paid more than a regular driver. (You don't want to take a chance on running over your high-priced show-biz cat, do you?)

And then there's the street. That's right. You can't just take your cast and crew out to the corner and start shooting. You need permits. You need to pay the owner of the location for permission to shoot there. You need to pay off-duty police officers to direct traffic around your crew.

That's why the line producer comes to you in the middle of prep. This stunt is killing us—can't we lose it? Well, no we can't. It's the most important thing in the entire story, because after the cat is run over it turns into a Hideous Drool Beast that's going to terrify the city.

The frustrated line producer goes away, but comes back an hour later. We found a stunt cat, but it will cost us five thousand dollars, because it's almost impossible to train a cat to walk under a car. On the other hand, we can get a dog for eight hundred. Can we make the switch?

Still no, because the cat is the reincarnation of Isis, an Egyptian goddess, and she's always represented by a cat.

The line producer pulls out a few more of his last remaining hairs and asks, What about the car? Can we make it a truck? Because then we can use one of our location vehicles and save a couple of bucks. Fine, you say, and you've saved your script.

Except that the next day the line producer comes back to you. It turns out there isn't a trained cat anywhere in L.A. County available for this episode. Can we toss a stuffed cat out and hope to hide it with quick cuts? Sure, but it will look like crap.

That's when the executive producer chimes in. Make it a dog. You start to object: But Isis—

No objections. The *dog* is now the reincarnation of Anubis, an Egyptian god represented by canines.

And since the gender switch is going to require a change on every page in the script, you'd better start writing.

This is the kind of thing that happens every day on a TV show—and it's the kind of writing they never teach you in film school. How do you do it? How do you make the compromises that are necessary to shoot your script without losing everything that made it good in the first place?

It's not that hard; well, sometimes it's not. But before you can start compromising, you need a firm understanding of what is essential to the script and what is disposable. That's the key, pure and simple. Know what your script is *about* and you'll know what you can lose, and what you have to keep.

Usually the first things to change are locations. When we turn in a script, we always expect to hear, "Can we move this scene to our standing sets? Can we take this scene off our standing sets and put it on the street?"

That's because of the rigors of scheduling a shoot. Keep in mind, an average TV drama has to film seven to twelve script pages per day. We can do that as long as we're efficiently scheduled. But let's say we have a scene that takes place in a toy store. It's three pages. Then we have two scenes that take place in a soda fountain, for a total of six pages. Neither location has enough scenes to fill a day. Granted, we could shoot the toy store, then move on. But that means setting up our equipment at the toy store, shooting for an hour or two, breaking down the equipment, loading it onto the trucks, driving the trucks to the new location, unloading the equipment, and setting it all up again. We could easily lose a quarter of the day.

Unless we move that toy store scene into the soda fountain. Or junk both locations in favor of a third that will handle all of our needs. Or just play it all on our standing sets (i.e., sets that are used in every episode, like the bridge of the *Enterprise* or the squad room in *Law & Order*).

Yes, but, you're saying. These scenes are specifically keyed to these locations. Of course they are, otherwise you wouldn't have set them there. But are the locations central to what the scenes are about, or are they just decoration?

There's an episode of *The West Wing* called "The Drop-In" in which Toby makes a major alteration in a speech Sam has written without telling him. Toward the episode's end, Sam is in Toby's office, yelling at him for doing this, and then he storms out, saying he doesn't want to talk to Toby anymore. In the next scene, Sam is in an upscale bar and Toby, beer in hand, is explaining himself, picking up the conversation just where it left off.

This doesn't really make a lot of sense. We just saw Sam storm out of Toby's office. Presumably, Sam went into the garage, got his car, and drove to the bar. Did Toby follow him all the way? Did they ride together, not speaking until they got there? What's going on?

Well, what's going on is this: There's another story in the same episode in which C. J. has a meeting in an upscale New York hotel lobby. This meeting takes place over two scenes, probably totaling no more than six or seven pages. It's not enough to fill a day, and it really does have to take place in the hotel.

Now let's take another look at that bar scene. The discriminating local eye will notice that the upscale bar in question is actually the bar at the Regal Biltmore, a five-second elevator ride from the location of C. J.'s meeting.

Odds are, the Toby/Sam scene originally was set in Sam's office, where it would make sense—Toby follows Sam in to finish the conversation. But doing that would have forced a different scene to be shot at the Biltmore, and there probably wasn't one that would work as well. So Aaron Sorkin writes a few lines of bar-location-specific dialogue and sets the scene there.

And you know what? It works. Because while it's not completely logical that they'd be having this conversation here, the scene isn't about the location, it's about the emotions of the two men and the demands that politics puts on their ideals. Where it plays is of no import.

But sometimes location is crucial. On our first year at *Diagnosis*

Murder we wrote a script that violated one of the chief rules of economic filmmaking—we set a two-page scene at one unduplicated location. And we made it one of the most expensive locations to shoot—the airport.

And to make matters worse, it was a scene that absolutely, positively could only take place at the airport. Oh, maybe we could make one small compromise—it could be *outside* the airport. Still a nightmare to shoot.

We knew this would cause problems, and it did. And in an effort to make the schedule work, we tried to move the scene somewhere else. Anywhere else. But it was the key scene of the show, and it only made sense if it took place at the airport.

Fortunately, our line producer, Barry Steinberg, and our director, Chris Nyby, are both brilliant when it comes to this kind of problem. Chris figured out a way to use long lenses, tight coverage, and lots of cars and extras with suitcases to transform the front of a hotel we were already shooting at into the exterior of LAX. But it took a lot of work (signs, airport shuttles, taxis, sound effects of planes lifting off, etc.) and a chunk of money, and we could only do it because we were able to show that in this case, the airport was the most essential element of the scene. And to make the schedule work, we had to move some other scenes around.

It's not only locations that get changed. Sometimes we'll write a story line for one regular character and then discover during prep that the actor who plays that character is going to be sick or otherwise unavailable during the shoot. What do we do? Sometimes it's just a matter of adjusting the scenes to make the story fit a different character. But sometimes the story in question only works for one character, and we need to hustle to come up with another storyline, one that uses the same basic locations and supporting actors, if we've already committed ourselves.

We had an episode of *Diagnosis Murder* with a subplot involving a European princess staying in the hospital and falling in love with Dick Van Dyke's character. It was a cute story line and dovetailed beautifully with the A story, which was about a master criminal plotting the princess' assassination as cover for a robbery. We were lucky enough to land Victoria Tennant to play the princess. And when we finished our prep week on Friday for a Monday shoot, we knew we were in great shape.

Until we turned on the TV late Saturday afternoon. Princess Diana had just been killed in a car crash.

Suddenly our cute story involving the possible death of a European princess didn't seem so cute. But we couldn't hold up production, and we certainly couldn't substitute a new script at this point. So we were in the office first thing Sunday morning putting out new pages, changing the princess into an heiress or a businesswoman or something. It worked—and we spent the week being grateful that we hadn't started shooting this a day or two earlier.

You always need to remain flexible when you're producing a TV show. No matter how perfectly your script might read, there are going to have to be changes. If you try to hold on to everything you wrote, you'll lose it all. You've got to find ways to protect the script's integrity, even if you lose many of the details.

It's easy to get into a bunker mentality at this point. You have this great script, and all these people want to screw it up. But of course that's not the case. They have to find a way to shoot as much of what you've written as they can. They're trying to help.

But just like people who are trying to help you with script notes, sometimes they're going to give you solutions instead of problems. You'll hear "we need to take Scenes 18 and 34 out of the standing sets and lose the car chase." But in your mind those two scenes can't play anywhere BUT the standing sets, and the car chase is the whole reason for doing this episode.

That's when you have to ask what problems they're facing. You'll find that what they really mean is there are eight pages too many scheduled for the standing sets and we're $5,000 over budget on stunts. And they've found a way to solve both problems.

You don't like their solution? Trust us, they won't object, as long as you come up with a better one. Instead of moving eight pages off the standing sets, let's take this four-page walk-and-talk from Fred's Bar and move it onto the standing sets, which gives us a full extra day in the studio and saves a location cost. And instead of losing the car chase, let's lose a couple of one-line day players and drop the bar fight in Act One (since we've already lost the bar), and that should pay for the $5,000 overage.

Of course, there are times when you've got to make script changes even if they hurt the episode. Sometimes, even if they ruin it.

You have to keep in mind that different shows have different needs and different priorities. If a high-end, top-rated drama like *The West Wing* or *The X-Files* runs into production trouble, they may well go a day or two over schedule. Most shows can't operate this way.

We were doing a syndicated action show called *Cobra* that was shot in Vancouver. There are a lot of advantages to shooting in the Pacific Northwest—not least of which is that (at the time anyway) it was substantially cheaper than doing it in L.A. And when your show has a budget under $650,000 per episode—less than a third of some network hours—cheaper means a lot.

Another great thing about Vancouver is that in the summer, the sun rises around five in the morning and doesn't go down until sometime next Tuesday, which gives you lots of daylight shooting time. The downside is that when winter rolls around, it's dark by four in the afternoon. And it rains. A lot.

We had an episode that involved some sneaky shenanigans at a military base. Honestly, the plot is a distant memory (although the title isn't: "A Few Dead Men." We still get a kick out of that.). But the entire fourth act consisted of some enormous action scene that was to take place during military maneuvers. Trucks, tanks, automatic weapons, bombs. It was going to be big.

Notice the verb tense. *Was going to be*. Because while we were prepping the episode, it started to rain. And rain. And rain. And while it was raining, the temperature started to drop into the low thirties. Did we mention this was January in Vancouver? The forest where we planned to shoot our action finale was a giant mud puddle. We couldn't even drive our trucks in there, for fear we couldn't get them back until summer.

And so we started to scramble for a new ending. Of course, we couldn't actually write the finale until we knew where it could be set—and there was *nowhere*. Our location people went crazy, working themselves near to death to find us a new spot for an action scene. But there were several other series shooting in Vancouver at the same time, as well as countless features, commercials, and music videos, and every location we went after was already taken. There was no good alternative.

Which is why, if you ever see *Cobra* showing up on some cable channel late one night, you'll get to the end of our incredible, military-themed episode and find the huge action finale taking place . . . in a high school gym.

Yup, a gym. Don't ask us what ridiculous plot contrivance got our heroes and villains there. We wrote this finale in the middle of the night in our hotel rooms and could barely remember it a week later, let alone ten years. Suffice it to say, it was terrible.

And it was necessary. If we'd shut down to wait for a location, it would have cost tens of thousands of dollars every day, and the company footing the bills wasn't going to pay that. Honestly, writing the new finale hurt us. The action at the end was the high point of the whole episode, and losing it meant, frankly, that the episode was going to be a stinker. But what was the option? Bankrupt the company? Get the series canceled? Quit?

There are times in television when you have to say, "This episode isn't going to work" and move on to the next one. Even the best shows on TV have one or two stinkers every year. And if you spend too much time trying to save the unsalvageable, you risk screwing up the next three. That's the great thing about series television—if your current episode is a disaster, there's always another one coming up to take its place. And this one will come out better.

Exercise

- Remember that beat sheet you rewrote for budget reasons in chapter 12? Well, you're not done yet. The actor playing the second lead character has the flu. Write him or her out of the episode and make the story work. How does the story change? How much of the story can you keep the same? What conflicts do you have to rework or abandon altogether? Or do you have to completely rejigger the plot and create new conflicts?

17

Your Really Great Idea for a Show

At a writing seminar we were giving in Miami, a lady in the audience stood up and declared that she wasn't going to waste her time doing all the hard work we suggested.

Writing a spec, pitching, freelancing, working your way up the producing ranks, it's all a pointless waste of time. She wasn't going to bother with it. She was going straight to running her own show.

We were intrigued. How was she going to do that?

All it takes, she told us, is a *Really Great Idea for a Show*. And she had one. Not only that, she'd already written the first eighteen episodes, scouted locations (conveniently all in her apartment building), and come up with a list of actors for the parts. Now all she had to do was sell her TV series, which she figured would be easy, since she'd already done all the work.

We told her she had a far better chance of being kidnapped by aliens, taken back to their home planet, and worshipped as a god.

We didn't mean to hurt her feelings (okay, maybe we did just a little bit), but she had to know the truth.

And so do you.

What she didn't know, and what most casual viewers of TV shows who think they can "do it better than those lousy writers" don't know either, is that a *Really Great Idea for a Show* is almost worthless. It's the execution of the idea that counts.

Or, to put it more succinctly: Ideas are cheap, execution is everything.

NYPD Blue is about cops in a precinct in New York. Big deal.

Hardly a *Really Great Idea for a Show*. But if Emmy winners Steven Bochco and David Milch want to do a series about police officers in a precinct in New York, that means something. It makes it a *Really Great Idea for a Show*.

Magnum, P.I. is not a great idea. It's just a private investigator in Hawaii. But that isn't what CBS bought. What the network bought was established showrunner Glen A. Larson writing and producing a show about a PI in Hawaii.

Let's say you've got a great story about homicide detectives in Baltimore. So what? Who is going to care? But when Oscar-winning director Barry Levinson had the same idea, NBC bought it immediately.

Why?

Because they were buying Barry Levinson's experience and successful track record first, the idea a distant second.

When the network buys a series, they are trusting you with $50 million. They have to believe that you know how to spend that money well, that you have the experience, the skills, and the talent to deliver new episodes on time and on budget every single week.

They aren't gonna give that lady in Miami $50 million, no matter how many scripts she's written.

But that didn't occur to her. TV was just something she watched, the shows just entertainment. She'd probably never given any thought to how those programs were actually made.

And that's why we wanted to hurt her feelings a little, because as stupid as it sounds, we were offended. Because what she was saying when she stood up and made that pronouncement was this: I've watched TV, it's not so hard. Anybody can do it. In fact, I can do it better than you can because I'm brighter than you are, because I did something you can't, I came up with a *Really Great Idea for a Show*.

What she was also saying was: I'm a complete idiot.

What she didn't realize is that television is a business like any other.

If you have a great idea for a frozen dinner, you can't just send Swanson your recipe and expect them to let you cook it. We can scrawl a drawing of a car right now on a napkin, but it would be ludicrous to believe that General Motors is going to pay us to build it.

So why would anyone believe that creating a TV show is any different?

If we were two guys from any other industry besides one in the arts, she never would have been as presumptuous.

Okay, so now you're thinking, there's still a shortcut. I'll just sell my brilliant idea to an executive producer and he'll make me rich.

A lot of people have this clever notion. We get unwanted pitches all of the time, and in the strangest places. For example, minutes before Bill's wedding, the rabbi pulled him aside to pitch his *Really Great Idea for a Show: Hear No Evil, See No Evil, Speak No Evil.* It was about three private eyes in business together. We'll let you guess what made each of them unique. Lee was having a proctology exam when the doctor started telling him his *Really Great Idea for a Show:* It was the thrilling story of a proctologist who was actually a suave international jewel thief.

The truth is, it's highly unlikely a producer will jump on your idea, even if you are joining him and his wife in holy matrimony or shoving a camera up his rectum when you suggest it.

We aren't going to buy your idea because the money for us is in our own ideas—unless, of course, you're asking us to adapt your best-selling novel or hit movie into a TV series, but that's a whole different matter (in fact, there *is* one shortcut to getting your own series, one that Aaron Sorkin and Kevin Williamson took: Simply write a movie that grosses a couple hundred million dollars, and the networks will come to *you*).

The opportunity to create a TV series is what every writer/producer is striving for, the chance to articulate your own creative vision instead of someone else's. The chance to not only write scripts and produce episodes, but also have a piece of the syndication, merchandising, and all the other revenue streams that come from being an *owner* and not an *employee*. The chance to become the next David E. Kelley, John Wells, J. J. Abrams, Stephen J. Cannell, Dick Wolf, Aaron Spelling, Donald Bellisario, Glen A. Larson, Steven Bochco, or one of the other members of that very small, very elite, very wealthy club of creator/owners.

So until you have the experience, or write that $100-million-grossing movie, what do you do with your *Really Great Idea for a Show?*

Stick it in a drawer.

Write your spec episode of *CSI.* Impress Dick Wolf with your spec and get an assignment to write an episode of *Law & Order: Special Victims Unit.* Get hired on staff, work your way up to producer. Quit and join *The Practice,* rise up to co-exec producer, and then, one day, the phone will ring. . . .

It will be someone at the network. A VP of Development. And that VP will have just one question for you: "Hey, got any ideas for a series?"

That's when you can open your drawer, whip out that *Really Great Idea for a Show* about the half-man/half-plant cop, and make your fortune.

So be patient. And have a very big drawer.

Exercise

- We know you have a *Really Great Idea for a Show.* Everybody does. But you can do something nobody else ever thinks about (unless they've read this book!): Take that great idea and apply everything you've learned in this book so far. What is the franchise? What are the central conflicts at the heart of the franchise? Are those conflicts complex and interesting enough to drive 100 or more episodes? Is your *Really Great Idea for a Show* fresh and different, and yet familiar enough to fit into mainstream television? If you still like the idea after answering those questions, stick it in the drawer to whip out when that network pitch meeting finally comes your way. You'll already be prepared to answer the tough questions the network execs will throw at you.

18

I'm a Professional Writer, and I've Got the Card to Prove It

We still remember the thrill of joining the Writers Guild of America and getting our membership cards in the mail.

That's when we knew we'd become professional writers.

It was a thrill matched only by the moment a few months later when we each received a green envelope in the mail, the one that contained our first residual check.

That's when we knew we might just make a living as professional writers.

But even before you join the WGA, you get to enjoy the major benefit of being a member: getting paid.

And not just when you write the script, but every time that episode is rerun.

Not only that, the producers and studios that hire you have to treat you like you're already a member.

Which means they have to pay you a minimum amount, currently around $27,000, for an hour-long teleplay.

Which means they can only demand a certain number of revisions before they have to pay you even more money.

Which means that thirty days after the show reruns on a network, they have to pay you a residual.

Which means that if you don't receive your money within certain amount of time, the Guild will assess penalties and interest on your behalf.

Great, huh?

And that's just the beginning. The studios have to do all of these things because the Guild negotiated those terms for *all* writers.

But you can't get away with enjoying the benefits for free for very long. After that first script sale, you're going to be invited—actually, it's more like an order—to join the Guild. There's an initiation fee of a couple thousand dollars, and you'll have to give them 1.5 percent of your income in dues each quarter, but it's money very well spent.

In many ways, they are like an extension of your agent. They won't find work for you, but they will do just about everything else.

If you get in a predicament with a producer, the Guild's legal staff will fight it for you. For example, we once had a dispute with a company we were working for. We were doing the work, but they weren't paying for it.

Despite our agent's nagging, threatening, and cajoling, they still wouldn't pay us. We didn't have to hire a lawyer for hundreds of dollars an hour to get our money. The Guild lawyers represented us for free. They got us our money, plus interest and penalties. And best of all, we didn't make any enemies doing it. We were insulated.

The Guild, like your agent, can get between you and your employer so you aren't put in the awkward position of fighting with someone you might want to work for again . . . even if they didn't pay you on time.

Hey, this is TV. You can't always afford to hold a grudge.

The Guild will also hunt down and collect your residuals and royalty payments when your show is broadcast, or sold on video or DVD, anywhere in the world.

But the Guild does more than just fight some of your battles and collect your money. They also protect your creative rights.

All the writing credits in Hollywood are determined by the Writers Guild—actually by a committee of your fellow writers, which is great. It's this practice that stops some studio exec from sticking his girlfriend's name on your script because she retyped the title page for him.

A writing credit that accurately reflects the contributions of the writers who did the work isn't just about ego. It's about money. Your percentage of the residual royalties is determined by what credit you get on-screen, which is one reason the power to determine those credits was taken away from the studios and given to the Guild.

Anytime a member of the writing staff of a show asks for credit, the credits are automatically arbitrated by the Writers Guild. What that means is that three anonymous writers will read the various drafts of the script (with the authors' names removed and replaced by "Writer A," "Writer B," etc.) and determine who should get credit, and in what form (story, teleplay, adaptation, etc.).

Credit arbitration is one of the most contentious, and important, functions the Guild provides to its members.

There's more: a great health care plan, a credit union, and pension plan.

But the Guild also gives you something less tangible, something that isn't reflected in your checkbook or tax return:

Membership in the Guild gives you a sense of belonging to something.

If you are out there freelancing, it is very lonely. But knowing you can go to the Guild and get involved in committee work or one of their social functions, helps you connect with other writers, establish contacts, and feel more plugged in to the industry and the writing life.

It also gives you the aura of professionalism. If you are a Writers Guild member, then you *are* a professional writer. No question about it.

Anyone can say they are a screenwriter.

Not everyone has a card that proves it.

Exercise

- Visit www.wga.org and familiarize yourself with the minimum basic agreement and the rules governing the relationship between writers and employers. If you're going to be a professional writer, you need to know your rights and responsibilities.

Afterword

We made our first sale to *Spenser: For Hire* in January 1987. Since then we've written or produced hundreds of hours of television. Some of it we look back on with pride. Some of it we look back on and wince. Some of it is *Baywatch*.

As long as there are struggling cable networks desperate to fill time between Bowflex infomercials, our work will continue to be seen by people around the world. And to be honest, sometimes, if the right mood strikes us, or we can't sleep, or we're just desperate to remember the 800 number for that free Bowflex video, we'll join that global audience watching our old shows.

But while we're tuned in to the same program as the rest of the world, we're not seeing the same thing. They're watching David Hasselhoff diving into the water or Dick Van Dyke exposing a murderer or Roy Scheider firing torpedoes at an enemy sub or Sammo Hung beating up three armed thugs with his necktie. We're seeing the moments, good and bad, hilarious and horrible, that went into the making of that episode. We're seeing scenes from our lives:

- Watching an entire cornfield set aflame by scorched airplane parts to simulate a plane crash . . . *just because we wrote it.*
- Standing on the Santa Monica Pier at dawn, watching a huge crew preparing to dump an armored car into the bay . . . *just because we wrote it.*
- Watching an entire building get blown to bits in a massive fireball . . . *just because we wrote it.*

- Standing on the curb as two cars careen around a street corner and slam through the window of a department store . . . *just because we wrote it.*
- Watching a team of ninja assassins rappel down the side of a towering L.A. skyscraper . . . *just because we wrote it.*
- Watching special effects artists labor for hundreds of hours to create a massive underwater battle between two submarines . . . *just because we wrote it.*
- Standing in the middle of the baggage claim area at Boston's Logan Airport, which a film crew had taken over and filled with a hundred fake passengers and hundreds of pieces of empty luggage . . . *just because we wrote it.*
- Watching (awkwardly and with much embarrassment) as two major TV stars stripped off their clothes and made love . . . *just because we wrote it.*

We could fill another book with memories like these. But out of all those years, all those episodes, there is one moment that right now stands out above all the others:

It was a blisteringly hot July afternoon. We were shooting a wedding scene in the backyard of an enormous Malibu estate, and the brilliant blue of the ocean and the flaming red of the bougainvillea made it look like something out of a painting by Alma-Tadema. The lawn was filled with beautiful young women in expensive dresses and handsome gentlemen in tuxedoes.

And we were there with our entire writing staff for one special moment, one short scene that was worth blowing off an entire afternoon's work.

The director called "Action!" and Dick Van Dyke ambled across the lawn with guest star Patrick Duffy. They were playing old friends, and Duffy's character made a joke about hiding the ottoman whenever Mark Sloan—Dick Van Dyke—came to visit. Mark gave that Dick Van Dyke laugh, turned, and, not seeing the dog lying on the ground, *did the Rob Petrie trip.*

The director yelled "Cut!," the extras burst into applause, and behind the camera, five experienced TV writers glowed with pleasure. In that moment, we were all Rob Petrie.

We hope we haven't scared you away from a career in television. (If we did, you weren't very serious about it in the first place.) What we wanted to show you is that there's more to writing for television than just writing a good script—it's about salesmanship, collaboration, and a knowledge of how the business works. We wanted the experience of reading this book to be like having lunch with two good friends in the business—two guys who would talk candidly with you about what television is really like, how you can break in, and how you can *stay* in. We hope we've succeeded—and that someday soon you will become *our* good friend in the business.

Plotting a Mystery: How We Wrote *Diagnosis Murder*

Every week on *Diagnosis Murder,* Dr. Mark Sloan is able to unravel a puzzling murder by using clever deductions and good medicine to unmask the killer.

We wish we could say that he's able to do that because of our astonishing knowledge of medicine, but it's not.

We're just writers.

We know as much about being a doctor as we do about being a private eye, a lifeguard, a submarine captain, or a werewolf—and we've written and produced TV shows about all of them, too.

What we do is tell stories. And what we don't know, we usually make up . . . or call an expert to tell us.

Writing mysteries is, by far, the hardest writing we've had to do in television. Writing a *medical* mystery is even harder. On most TV shows, you can just tell a good story. With mysteries, a good story isn't enough, you also need a challenging puzzle. It's twice as much work for the same money.

We always begin developing an episode the same way. We come up with an "arena," the world in which our story will take place: a UFO convention; a murder in a police precinct, a rivalry between a mother and a daughter for the love of a man. Once we have the arena, we talk about the characters: Who are the people the story will be about? What makes them interesting? What goals do they have, and how do they conflict with the other characters?

And then we ask ourselves the big questions—who gets

murdered, how is he or she killed, and why? How we solve that murder depends on whether we are writing an open or closed mystery.

Whether the murder is "open," meaning the audience knows whodunit from the start, or whether it is "closed," meaning we find out who the killer is the same time that the hero does, is dictated by the series concept. *Columbo* mysteries are always open, *Murder She Wrote* is always closed, and *Diagnosis Murder* mixes both. An open mystery works when both the murderer and the audience think the perfect crime has been committed. The pleasure is watching the detective unravel the crime and finding the flaws you didn't see. A closed mystery works when the murder seems impossible to solve, and the clues that are found don't seem to point to any one person, but the hero sees the connection you don't and unmasks the killer with it.

In plotting the episode, the actual murder is the last thing we explore, once we've settled on the arena and devised some interesting characters. Once we figure out who to kill and how, then we start asking ourselves what the killer did wrong. We need a number of clues, some red herrings that point to other suspects, and some clues that point to our murderer. The hardest clue is the finish clue (or as we'll call it, the "ah-ha!"), the little shred of evidence that allows the hero to solve the crime—but still leaves the audience in the dark.

The finish clue is the hardest part of writing a *Diagnosis Murder* episode, because it has to be something obscure enough that it won't make it obvious who the killer is to everybody, but definitive enough that the audience will be satisfied when we nail the murderer with it.

A *Diagnosis Murder* episode is a manipulation of information, a game that's played on the audience. Once you have the rigid frame of the puzzle, you have to *hide* the puzzle so the audience isn't aware they are being manipulated. It's less about concealment than it is about distraction. If you do it right, the audience is so caught up in the conflict and drama of the story that they aren't aware that they are being constantly misdirected.

The difficulty, the sheer, agonizing torture, of writing *Diagnosis Murder* is telling a good story while at the same time constructing a challenging puzzle. To us, the story is more important than the puzzle—the show should be driven by character conflict, not our need to reveal clues. The revelations should come naturally out of character, because people watch television to see interesting people in interesting situations, not to solve puzzles. A mystery without the character and story isn't very entertaining.

In our experience, the best "ah-ha!" clues come from character, not from mere forensics; for instance, we discover Aunt Mildred is the murderer because she's such a clean freak that she couldn't resist doing the dishes after killing her nephew.

But this is a series about a doctor who solves crimes. Medicine has to be as important as character-based clues. So we try to mix them together. The medical clue comes out of character.

So how do we come up with that clever bit of medicine?

First, we decide what function or purpose the medical clue has to serve and how it is linked to our killer; then we make a call to an expert to help us find the right malady, drug, or condition that fits our story needs. If one of our paid medical consultants doesn't know the answer, we go to the source. If it's an episode about infectious diseases, for instance, we might call the Centers for Disease Control. If it's a forensic question, we might call a medical examiner. If it's a drug question, we'll call a pharmaceutical company. It all depends on the story. And more often than not, whoever we find is glad to answer our questions.

For instance, in one episode there's a terrible bus accident and the passengers are trapped inside. Once they are freed, paramedics discover one of the passengers is dead. What Dr. Mark Sloan discovers is that the accident didn't kill the passenger—the man was murdered. The killer had to be one of the passengers, since they were all trapped inside the bus after the accident. So someone killed the person in the five minutes after the accident and before the paramedics arrived and hoped the death would be blamed on the crash.

We knew we needed a medical clue that Dr. Sloan could find that would reveal the man's death was actually murder, not a result of the bus crash. So we called our medical consultant, Dr. Gus Silva, and gave him the details. He called some of his fellow doctors and got back to us an hour later with the forensic clues we needed.

One of the paramedics in the episode is cocky, self-confident, and studying for med school entrance exams. Dr. Sloan, to help her out, gives her a pop quiz, asking her four questions. She gets one of them wrong, but Dr. Sloan won't tell her which one because he wants her to figure it out for herself.

We thought it would be clever if Dr. Sloan realizes she made the same mistake committing the murder that she makes in his pop quiz . . . in other words, her mistake comes from the same cockiness and overconfidence she demonstrates in her zeal to become a doctor. We went ahead and plotted the story, but relied on Dr. Silva to get back to us with just the right subtle medical mistake that would trip up the paramedic.

We also tricked the viewer. By repeatedly having Mark Sloan say "the murder must have occurred after the accident and before the paramedics showed up," we imposed a way of looking at the situation on the audience. We made it seem as if the paramedics were excluded from suspicion . . . so that when we *did* reveal that the killer was a paramedic, it was a surprise. We never thought of the paramedic as a suspect because we were, in effect, told not to. Mark was operating under a false assumption, and so were we. Offering the audience a misleading framework for interpreting the facts is a common tool, known as "misdirection," in plotting a mystery.

The viewers enjoy the game as long as you play fair, and as long as they feel they had the chance to solve the mystery, too. Even if they do solve it ahead of your detective, if it was a difficult and challenging mystery, they feel smart and don't feel cheated. They are satisfied, even if they aren't surprised.

If Dr. Sloan catches the killer because of some arcane medical fact you'd have to be an expert to catch, then we've failed and you won't watch the show again.

The medical clue has to be clever, but it can't be so obscure that you don't have a chance to notice it for yourself, even if you aren't an M.D. And it has to come out of character, so that even if you do miss the clue, it's consistent with, and arises from, a character's behavior you can identify.

To play fair, all the clues and discoveries have to be shared with the audience at the same time that the hero finds them. There's nothing worse than withholding clues from the audience—and the sad thing is, most mysteries on television do it all the time. The writers do it because playing fair is much, much harder than cheating. If you have the hero get the vital information offscreen, during a commercial, the story is a lot easier to plot and the writing staff can eat out for lunch instead of having pizza delivered again . . . and being stuck in a story conference for six more hours.

But when a *Diagnosis Murder* episode works, when the mystery is tight and the audience is fairly and honestly fooled, it makes all the hours of painful plotting worthwhile.

That, and the residual check.

Diagnosis Murder
Writers' Guidelines

Just about everything you need to know about the show you will find from reading the scripts and viewing the episodes we've given you. But here are some basics:

We are a mystery series. We always have a murder. And usually there is a medical clue that plays a major role in solving the crime. But that's it. Beyond that, we have no formula. We don't want to be *Murder, She Wrote*. We want to play with the form and have some fun. There's enough flexibility in our format, and with our characters, to do dramas and comedies, and to tell mysteries in new and interesting ways.

The star of our show is Dick Van Dyke. He has many talents, and we encourage you to use them. But don't resurrect old routines from the Dick Van Dyke show or movies that he's done—this is a new character (okay, well, not all that new after more than 100 episodes).

Play fair with our audience. They love mysteries and want to try and solve them with Mark. Never hide clues from the audience. Mark never discovers something during a commercial or off-camera that he will use to nail the bad guy. Assume the viewers are taping the show and when it's over, will rewind the tape to see what clues they missed. And if they never had the chance to solve the mystery themselves, they will feel cheated.

Although we have to do a few classic whodunits each season (a murder, four suspects, one of them did it) and *Columbo*-esque open mysteries (you see a guy commit the perfect murder and then watch as Mark Sloan uncovers his mistakes), we try to find a way to give them a unique twist so they don't seem so formulaic: solving a murder in the midst of a raging forest fire; assigned to the NTSB strike team investigating a 747 crash; solving a murder while locked in quarantine and infected with a deadly disease; solving a murder entirely in flashback; solving a murder that began twenty years ago on *Mannix,* and so on.

We like medical clues, but we prefer to nail our bad guys with clues that come from behavior, habit, or personal quirks. We never catch a bad guy from fingerprints, DNA, or easy forensic stuff like that. Usually it's a combination of a medical clue, a behavior, and a mistake. We'd give examples here, but they just don't play out of context. The best thing to do is just read the scripts and storylines.

We want you to write tight, interesting dialogue and move the story along swiftly. That said, our scripts are typically sixty-eight to seventy pages long. Mark Sloan appears in no more than thirty-two to thirty-five pages, due to Dick Van Dyke's work schedule. We shoot in seven days, and we like to have at least two or three days on our standing sets: the hospital, the police station, and Mark Sloan's beach house. We like action but we don't have the budget for much, so be judicious with it. Forget about that big automatic weapons shootout in hot air balloons over downtown L.A., and the screeching car chase down the Pacific Coast Highway.

The Characters

Dr. Mark Sloan (Dick Van Dyke) is the chief of internal medicine at Community General Hospital and a consultant to the LAPD. His son Steve (Barry Van Dyke) is a homicide detective. They live together at Mark's Malibu beach house. Mark also has an estranged daughter, Carol, who lives in northern California

Mark and Steve work closely with Dr. Amanda Bentley (Victoria Rowell), a pathologist at Community General and an adjunct county medical examiner. She performs autopsies for both the county and the hospital out of her pathology lab at the hospital. She is often called to the scenes of murders before Mark or Steve show up. She's divorced and the mother of a four-year-old son named C. J. Amanda comes from a wealthy family and is well educated, bright, and very self-confident.

Dr. Jesse Travis (Charlie Schlatter) is a resident in the Community General emergency room and something of a second son to Mark Sloan. He really admires the relationship Mark and Steve have, something he wishes he could have with his own father, Dane Travis, whom he has rarely seen since his parents divorced. That's because, as Jesse learned recently, his father was an intelligence agent working abroad. Jesse is an extremely competent and capable doctor, though he's only an apprentice when it comes to investigating crimes. He's also involved in a romantic relationship with a young nurse, Susan Hilliard (Kim Little). Jesse replaced Dr. Jack Stewart, played in the first few seasons of the show by Scott Baio.

Cat-and-Mouse Scenes

The "investigatory" scenes in which Mark questions suspects, our "cat-and-mouse" scenes," are the hardest scenes in any episode to write (and yet, usually, the best in the episode). While it's necessary for Mark to get a lot of information from his target, it has to be done almost effortlessly, without Mark seeming to "question" the person. He prefers to catch them off guard, so they are giving him stuff without them even realizing they are being interrogated. Mark manipulates these situations—he never comes across as an accuser or questioner but just as an interested party. This is Mark Sloan's charm—and his greatest strength as an investigator. It's also easy to fall into mimicking Columbo, which we don't want to do. Mark has his own style, his own humor—he's Dick Van Dyke, after all, and we want to take advantage of his many talents.

Our Big Finales

Getting out the clue details at the end of the show is always hard, but it should also be the most satisfying scene in the script. This is, after all, the moment we're always building toward. It should be fun. And Mark Sloan takes great pleasure in this—it's probably the reason why he's a detective at all.

The trick is getting all the clues and explanation out dramatically (or humorously), without Mark basically giving a speech, interrupted by such wonderful lines from the suspect as: "What are you talking about?," "You're crazy," and "This is ridiculous." Easy automatic lines like those don't *reveal* character, move the story forward, or throw Mark off in the least. We need to make these finales a dialogue, not a speech. Mark is talking with, not to, the suspect. Give our killers an attitude; the suspect should refute the accusations, show faults in Mark's reasoning, so Mark can best him or her. Otherwise it's no fun; it's just a lecture from Mark.

The Bottom Line

We don't want to be the old, tired *Murder, She Wrote* knockoff people thought we were (and rightly so). The last two seasons, we have fought hard to change the industry and popular perception of the show, and we have succeeded—now the show gets glowing coverage in the press and has shot into the top thirty. To stay there we need you, your fresh stories, and, above all, your enthusiasm.

If you have any questions as you prepare your pitch, please do not hesitate to contact one of us. Good luck!

Martial Law Writers' Guidelines

This is not a cop show.

It's an action-adventure comedy that delivers the kind of thrills and fun that, until now, you had to pay $7.50 to see. It's a throwback, in the best sense of the word, to the kind of sixties television we all loved as kids—*The Wild Wild West, I Spy, The Avengers, The Man from U.N.C.L.E.*—but with a contemporary spin and the kind of martial arts action that only Sammo Hung and Stanley Tong can deliver. We want to capture the wild, unpredictable action of the best Hong Kong movies and the character comedy of films like *48 Hours* and *Lethal Weapon*.

Our stories are not about crimes, suspects, and clues, they are about fun, comedy, and pure adrenaline. Our stories should never stop moving and should leave the viewer exhilarated. If the story you have in mind can be done on any other show, then it's dead wrong for *Martial Law*.

As far as we are concerned, last season didn't exist. We aren't sticking to any of the backstory, with the exception of the central concept: a cop from China working on the L.A. police force as part of an exchange program.

Here are some basics:

Each episode should start hot. That doesn't mean it has to begin with Sammo Hung in a martial arts sequence, but it does mean we want a strong hook, something the viewers can't resist. Big action is a plus, but as long as the teaser really grabs you, that's all that's important.

The stories should put our heroes in conflict. We aren't saying they should be constantly bickering, arguing and fighting, but they should have differing opinions and approaches to the problems they have to resolve. That's a big part of the fun—seeing how they are different from each other and what makes them unique. But remember, these people genuinely like each other and the disagreements aren't personal. The paradigm here is Captain Kirk, Mr. Spock, and Dr. McCoy . . . or James T. West and Artemus Gordon . . . or Murtaugh and Riggs.

Our heroes should have something at stake in every story. That doesn't mean we want to see their family members and friends as either the victims or the bad guys, nor does that mean one of our heroes has to be captured and facing death each week. That's the easy way out.

While each episode should have some major martial arts sequences, there is no formula. We don't have to have one at the end of each act, or necessarily one as our finale. Nor does each episode have to end with Sammo and the bad guy duking it out. Let the story dictate where the fights are, who they are with, and how long they have to be. We don't want the fights to feel irrelevant, tacked on or obligatory. And our heroes shouldn't always win; our guys can, and should, lose.

Each story should have a major turn at the end of Act Two—and if you can find major turns for the ends of Acts One and Three, we won't object. The last thing any of our plots should be is predictable. If we know the whole story in Act One, then it's not a story we should be doing.

The crime, whatever it is, should never be ugly or seamy. This isn't a show about kids killed in drive-by shootings, pregnant women getting raped, or anything else that makes your skin crawl and stomach turn. This show is an escape, not a dark reality. If it's not fun, we don't do it.

It's not funny, interesting, or unusual to put Sammo in his own element, helping other Chinese people in Chinatown, for instance. The fun comes when he's plunged into a cultural situation he doesn't understand. It's a lot more interesting to see him help some Hasidic

Jews in the Fairfax district than a Chinese family fighting to keep their restaurant.

Terrell will never, ever have a gun kicked out of his hand again. We don't make our martial artists look better by making our other heroes look stupid, weak, or ineffective.

We aren't interested in clues and suspects. That said, our detectives are smart. We need to see them being clever, intuitive, and experienced. We don't want them relying on easy clues like fingerprints, DNA, and forensic stuff. That can be a starting point, but we like to nail our bad guys using clues that come from behavior, habit, or personal quirks.

Not everyone in Los Angeles is a martial arts expert—if they were, Sammo wouldn't be unique. This is especially true of our villains. They don't all have to be Van Damme. If Sammo takes on a martial arts master, everybody knows exactly what they're going to get. But if he's unarmed and facing a bad guy with an Uzi, or a bomb, or a tank, then it gets interesting.

The Characters (An Overview)

Sammo Law (Sammo Hung) is a Shanghai cop on loan to the LAPD as part of an exchange program. He is a member of an elite major crime unit that works on high-profile cases and international crime, and that operates outside the usual LAPD bureaucracy. He's a good cop and a deceptively agile fighter—and always a fish out of water. No matter how long he lives in Los Angeles, he will always be thoroughly Chinese, and a lot of the fun in this series will come from the clashes between Sammo and American culture (and the many subcultures within our own).

His partner is Terrell Parker (Arsenio Hall), a tough, streetwise detective whose unpredictability makes him dangerous, not only to the crooks, but to everyone around him. His improvisational approach to crime fighting makes him a stark contrast to Sammo—and, in fact, to just about every other police officer on the force. Terrell is as much an outsider on the force as Sammo is to American culture. The difference is, Terrell totally understands the way things are done—he just chooses to do it differently.

The other members of the unit are Grace Chen (Kelly Hu), a fiercely independent Chinese American undercover cop and Sammo's former student, and Amy Dylan, the most decorated female cop in the department, whose ambition is only matched by her tireless dedication to her job.

The major crimes unit is for people who don't fit in anywhere else in the department, but are too damn good to let go—it allows them the space they need to do their best work. They are the American police equivalent of the British "flying squad." This unit doesn't only react to crimes that have already occurred; they are aggressive about preventing crimes before they happen. They will often target and bring down major criminal operations through undercover work, scams, traps, whatever it takes.

The Characters (The Nitty-Gritty)

Sammo Law

In Shanghai, Sammo Law was Columbo—with fists of fury. His intuitive and deductive skills were legendary, as was his amazing physical prowess. He was the perfect person to send to the United States as part of a high-level exchange of law enforcement experts. And for Sammo, it was a challenge he couldn't resist. What he wasn't prepared for are the huge cultural differences between the two countries and the impact they will have on how he works.

Sammo is smart, Sammo is funny, Sammo is charming, Sammo is surprisingly graceful . . . but most important, Sammo is Chinese. That doesn't mean (as it has in the past) that he speaks in fortune-cookie aphorisms and calls people "acorns." It means he comes with a completely different set of cultural assumptions. He believes in consensus and the success of his unit over his personal success, for instance. He prizes harmony between people and dislikes open confrontation. (Except with bad guys, of course.) He's much more comfortable with silence than his American partners. And he's been taught from birth never to let his personal feelings show.

There's a constant contrast between his methods of working and those around him. His idea of American law enforcement techniques comes from *T. J. Hooker* reruns; their idea of the Chinese police comes from bad movies. L.A. cops think he must be some kind of fascist interrogator who beats confessions out of everyone. Both sides have a lot of learning to do and a lot of preconceptions to abandon. (Sammo, for instance, doesn't use handcuffs—he'll use whatever is nearby. He might bind a suspect's thumbs together with a rubber band, or tangle his limbs around a simple stick, or wrap him around a light pole.)

This cultural difference applies to all areas of Sammo's life, not just law enforcement. For example, Sammo is far more careful with his money than most Americans and thinks about every nickel he spends. He's not cheap; he's just frugal. He has a very different conception of the proper social distance between people, often standing too close for American taste. Bribery might be an accepted way of doing business in China, and Sammo is still learning that it's frowned upon here—especially when a cop does it. He's not a prude, but he's not comfortable with public displays of affection or passion. There are a million differences between Shanghai's culture and ours, and Sammo runs into them every day.

But he doesn't let that, or his difficulty with English, slow him down. His deductive and reasoning skills transcend cultural differences. The fact is, he didn't communicate what he was thinking much in China, and now he can use his problems with English as an excuse to do it even less. In fact, he's happy to let people underestimate him—like Columbo, he finds that if his adversaries think he's stupid (or old or fat or incapable of understanding English), they're going to let down their guard and make mistakes in front of him. Sammo knows how good he is; he never feels compelled to prove it to anyone, especially if looking bad will help him reach his goals.

Besides, it has always been easier for him to just go out and do things his way, rather than waste time explaining himself, even if that gets him in more trouble here than it ever did in Shanghai. And when he does speak, it's not unusual for him to get colloquialisms or metaphors wrong, or at least very muddled ("I've got other cats on the griddle," "Don't pull my tongue," and so on.)

He is very much the classic fish out of water, and he will never entirely fit in. He's inquisitive about everything, almost like a child. And although he is a martial arts expert, he's not anxious to get into fights—he will use the least amount of force necessary to get the job done. He fights as a last resort, and he never uses a gun. He's the Chinese MacGyver of self-defense. Anything around him is a potential weapon, from a loaf of bread to a shelf of videocassettes, from an apron to a folding chair.

He is the de facto leader of the unit, but he doesn't press this point. Sammo is utterly self-effacing, with a wit so dry, it's sometimes hard to tell when he's joking. He has the utmost respect for his co-workers, even if he often disagrees with their approach. This is especially true with Terrell, his partner. Terrell talks fast, Sammo talks slow, or not at all. Terrell likes to argue a point into the ground; when Sammo disagrees, often he will communicate his unhappiness only with silence. Sammo communicates little, Terrell communicates too much. Sammo is low-key, Terrell is showy. Sammo plans, Terrell improvises. Their differences drive them both nuts.

Sammo still sees himself as a mentor to Grace, even if she doesn't. It's hard for him to accept that she's on her own now, making her own decisions. In a way, he's like a father who won't let go of his child, and she's like a daughter rebelling against a parent. In Sammo's mind, she is a capable detective and a promising martial artist who has become too Americanized in her thinking. Yet she is the one person who truly understands him.

Sammo and Grace have their own language, beyond Chinese, almost like a code. They can read each other's expressions and body language. All he has to do is breathe a certain way, and it can piss Grace off. (Grace: "You are so judgmental." Sammo: "I didn't say anything." Grace: "I heard you breathe!" Sammo: "I have a cold." Now, for the rest of the episode, he has to remember to pretend he has a cold so he doesn't hurt her feelings.) And they have a shared history, which they can refer to when dealing with a situation.

In Amy Dylan, he sees a woman with enormous potential if she would only relax, both physically and mentally. He takes her on as his new student, but it's going to take a lot of work.

Terrell Parker

He loves this job. He loves the danger. The car chases. The fights. And especially the expense account. There is no legal way to have this much fun, which is why he's wearing a badge.

Terrell likes nice clothes, fast cars, and women. Why be a cop otherwise? He's not in it strictly for law and order. He's a risk junkie, living for the high that comes from danger.

His weapons of choice are his smooth tongue and natural charm. If that doesn't work, he pulls out a gun. He can talk his way through just about anything, although he's not afraid to get tough when he has to. Terrell is not a martial artist, he's a street fighter. He fights hard, and he fights dirty, usually with the same flair for improvisation that characterizes everything else he does. That said, in a fair fight with someone larger than him, he will lose. So he doesn't fight fair. He would rather shoot someone or hit him from behind with a two-by-four than fight for twenty minutes.

He works on instinct and adrenaline, improvisation and pure luck—and knows he looks good doing it. He enjoys taking bows after a job well done, sometimes even before. His arrest record is among the best in the department, even if he can't seem to "play well with others." Terrell was booted from every division in the department before ending up in this major crimes unit. This is his last chance to make it, or he's finished as a cop.

No matter what, Terrell always knows he's on top of every situation. Usually he's right. Usually. He doesn't like to plan ahead, but prefers to go with the moment, to improvise, which often frustrates Sammo and irritates everyone else in the unit, especially Amy. But it's his unpredictability that is, in many ways, what makes him an exceptional cop.

Terrell loves what he does, and he wants to have a good time doing it. And he wants everybody else to have a good time, too. Which is one thing that really bugs him about his partner, Sammo. Why can't Sammo just loosen up? Terrell's always working to get some kind of reaction out of Sammo. What he doesn't realize is that this only makes Sammo more determined not to show him any-thing—Sammo's enjoying himself in ways that Terrell will never understand.

Grace finds Terrell too showy and is afraid his rogue approach could get them all killed. That is why she prefers to work alone, and why Terrell enjoys needling her so much. In his mind, she's too seri-ous, too full of herself, too much of a loner. And a very easy target for his own amusement.

Amy, on the other hand, represents everything Terrell dislikes about the department and why, until now, he hasn't really thrived. She is far too absorbed in the politics and procedures of the LAPD, too interested in promotion, in how things look to others, rather than just doing whatever it takes to get the job done. But even he can't deny her abilities.

Grace Chen

She's equal parts Emma Peel, La Femme Nikita, and even more Jen-nifer Lopez in *Out of Sight*. She's comfortable with her weapons, whether it's the ones she was born with—her fists, her feet, and her beauty—or the arsenal at her disposal.

She's happiest when she's undercover, freed from the restrictions and expectations others have placed on her, and that she's placed on herself. Alone, there's no one to disappoint but herself, and she rarely does that.

When she's with Sammo, she's like a sixteen-year-old trying to rebel against her strict father, a man she nonetheless respects and is utterly devoted to. What she can't seem to make him understand is that things are different here. She's knows more about America than he does. What he does may work in China, but it doesn't always work here.

Everyone else may see her as a lethal lady, but Sammo will always see her as a wayward student who still has many lessons left to learn. To him, she doesn't know more about America, she's just gotten sloppy. He sees it as his responsibility to reinforce in her the Chinese way of doing things. And that makes her crazy. Despite all that, they are very close. She is the one person he will open up to, because she is the only person in America who truly understands him.

Where Terrell is instinctive, she is aggressive. She always believes she is tougher than anyone in the room and wants to prove it. Although, like Terrell, she likes to do things her own way, she thinks things through. She never improvises, she strategizes constantly. The truth is, she wishes she had his skill for quick thinking, for choosing the one approach that would never occur to anyone else.

While Amy is an expert at politics, Grace is a total failure. Grace doesn't care about what's politically correct, only what works for her. While Amy wants to work within the system, Grace fights it. Grace rebels against anything that forces her to conform, that makes her less unique and independent. But again, the truth is she wishes she had Amy's ability to smoothly navigate the political waters of any situation.

What Grace is out to do is prove herself—to herself.

Amy Dylan

At twenty-six, she's the fastest-rising female cop in the history of the department. She got that way by being single-minded about her work, absolutely dedicated to her job, some would say obsessed.

Her goal is to be the first female police chief in LAPD history. To get there, she knows she has to not only be good, but better than everybody else. She will play the politics of any situation—and believes that this so-called promotion to the unit was actually designed by her male superiors to derail her rise to the top. To her, this is a demotion. She believes she's only one big arrest away from getting back into Robbery-Homicide and the promotion track.

As a result, she's relentless when it comes to pursuing a case and making sure it's done if not by the book, then within the boundaries of acceptable procedure. It's for her own protection. If they break all the rules to make a bust, and the judge throws the case out, they've wasted their time, returned a crook to the streets, and tarnished their careers.

Because she comes from a wealthy family, she can afford all the latest technology (even if the department can't), and is forever looking for any gadget that can give her an edge.

She talks to Sammo, Terrell, and Grace as if she is the only adult, and they are unruly children when the fact is that they actually have more experience than she does. Sammo has no desire to show her up—unlike Terrell and especially Grace, who will rub Amy's nose in a mistake every chance she gets. It's the one thing Grace and Terrell can always agree on.

Amy admires Sammo and Terrell; if only she could convince them to work within the system, they could be terrific cops. And she wishes she had Grace's ability to blend into any situation. No matter how hard Amy tries to blend in, no matter how she dresses, no matter how she walks, you can still always tell she's a cop.

Maybe that's because she *is* all cop. That is her life. What she lacks in physical prowess she more than makes up for with sharp intellect and political savvy. And she's smart enough to know this, which is why she swallowed her pride and asked Sammo to teach her martial arts. He gladly accepted because she recognizes this weakness in herself. The problem is, she's not proving to be a very good student. When it comes to martial arts, and Chinese teaching, she has a long way to go. She thinks her problem is physical prowess, but Sammo knows it's more about the way she thinks, which is too much. He will use martial arts to teach her not only how to fight, but how to find her true self.

What They All Have in Common

Despite their differences, they genuinely like and respect each other, and together make an extraordinary team. Although they may argue, although they may have different approaches, their basic respect and affection for one another never wavers.

Martial Law Pitch/Leave-Behind ("Sammo Blammo")

Here's a typical story area/leave-behind for *Martial Law*. You'll notice we didn't deal with the character conflicts that would be running through the story, just the conflict that drives the episode. That's fine if you're a producer trying to sell the network on the story, but not if you're a freelancer trying to convince a producer to give you an an assignment. The network takes it on faith that the character conflicts will be spelled out in the beat sheet, but a producer won't grant a freelancer the same benefit of the doubt.

MARTIAL LAW
"Sammo Blammo"
Story Area by
Lee Goldberg and William Rabkin

The story opens with our heroes narrowly thwarting the latest in a string of serial bombings. But it's not easy . . . and before it's over, Sammo has to fight off the terrorists while holding a bomb that will detonate if it doesn't remain level.

News of the bust is especially interesting to DANIEL DARIUS, an explosives expert who was just released from prison after spending fifteen years for a daring robbery that netted $100 million that's never been recovered.

Only problem is, Daniel doesn't know where it is. He was caught, and his cohorts weren't. He didn't even know who they were, or who the mastermind of the robbery was. Now he wants to find them . . . and get his share of the money. With interest. To do that, he'll need a shrewd detective and incredible resources. He's going to use Sammo and the major crimes unit to do the work for him.

Sammo hasn't slept in a day, and he's bushed. Maybe that's why Daniel is somehow able to overpower him. Daniel straps a small but elaborate bomb to his body . . . if Sammo doesn't keep moving, the bomb will explode. If it's tampered with in any way, it will explode. The only way to diffuse it is with an encrypted disc that only Daniel has.

Exhausted Sammo has twenty-four hours to find the crooks, the $100 million, and give Daniel his share—and keep moving—or it's Sammo blammo!

Martial Law Beat Sheet ("Sammo Blammo")

After the network approved the story area/leave-behind, we wrote up the beat sheet. While the beat sheet follows the broad strokes of the story area/leave-behind that the network approved, there were some significant changes. This episode ended up becoming the second season premiere and introduced new characters, relationships, and conflicts not anticipated when the original story was conceived.

MARTIAL LAW
"Sammo Blammo"
Revised Outline
Written by
Lee Goldberg and William Rabkin

TEASE

1. EXT. OIL REFINERY – NIGHT
Two CARS almost collide as they speed in from DIFFERENT DIRECTIONS. SAMMO LAW and TERRELL PARKER jump out of one car as another detective, AMY DYLAN, jumps out of the other. She is furious—what are they doing here? Terrell says they're closing in on the serial bombers who have been terrorizing the city. Amy says that's her investigation, no one authorized them to get involved. Terrell says since they are on the major crimes unit, they authorized themselves. She doesn't want anyone making a move until backup arrives. Terrell argues with her, purposely distracting

her and letting Sammo slip away. Actually, Sammo goes right over her head . . . scaling the pipes above them with incredible agility.

2. INT. OIL REFINERY – NIGHT

Sammo creeps around until he discovers THE BAD GUYS about to plant their bomb. The LEADER tells his sexy Asian babe girlfriend (hidden behind a pair of cool sunglasses) that when the bomb blows, it will cause a chain reaction that will ignite the entire complex and create a massive disaster. That's when the pipe Sammo is straddling SNAPS—and he plunges down in middle of the terrorists. Sammo identifies himself as a police officer and orders them to freeze. The LEADER tosses Sammo the bomb. Sammo instinctively catches it . . . and hears a click. The bomb is activated. If the bomb doesn't remain perfectly level, it explodes. Sammo glances at the BABE, who suddenly spin-kicks the two guys next to her. The glasses come off and we see she's actually GRACE CHEN, undercover! The fight is on, with Sammo trying not to tip the bomb. They defeat the bad guys just as Terrell and Amy rush in with the bomb squad. And on Sammo, standing perfectly still, an explosive in his hand, we FADE OUT.

END OF TEASE

ACT ONE

1. INT. OIL REFINERY – MORNING

It's now swarming with PRESS, who are kept at bay by UNI-FORMED OFFICERS. We CLOSE IN to FIND Sammo right where we left him, still standing, as JAKE CRAGG, grizzled leader of the bomb squad, tries to defuse the bomb in Sammo's hand. Meanwhile, Amy is giving Terrell and Grace hell. Sammo would not be in this position if they hadn't intruded into her investigation. Grace says she has been undercover with this terrorist cell for a month . . . revealing that to anyone else could have blown her cover. Amy isn't swayed. She believes the department made a big mistake letting the three of them splinter off into their own Major Crimes Unit when Capt. Winship retired and Louis transferred to the NYPD. What they need is someone to rein them in before people get hurt. She marches off.

Cragg defuses the bomb and an exhausted Sammo finally gets to move after hours of remaining still. Terrell tells Sammo he was the lead story on every newscast last night and is bound to be a headline this morning. Sammo doesn't care. All he wants to do now is go to bed. But he pauses on the way to whisper to Grace, "Why did you kick the men?" Because, she replies, you gave me the look. He says I didn't give you the look. She says yes you did. He says I gave you a glance, not a look. She says I definitely saw The Look. He says that's what happens when you wear sunglasses at night.

Sammo leaves. Or at least he starts to. . . .

2. EXT. OIL REFINERY – MORNING
Sammo is on his way to his car when he passes an OPEN VAN and a UNIFORMED OFFICER, who motions him over to sign a document. Just as Sammo leans down to look at the paper, the officer SPRAYS HIM IN THE FACE with something . . . Sammo starts to collapse, the officer pushes him into the van, slams the doors shut and DRIVES OFF.

3. INT. MAJOR CRIMES UNIT (MCU) – DAY
Terrell and Grace are about to leave when Amy come storming in, furious. She hands each of them a SHEAF of PAPERS: forms they must fill out before leaving. Terrell tosses them in the trash. Amy pulls them back out and shoves them into Terrell's hands. I went to the brass and registered an official complaint against your unit, she says. I told them someone had to make you accountable for your actions, remind you three that you are part of a police department, not independent contractors. I should have kept my mouth shut, she says ruefully. They made me that someone.

Terrell and Grace share a horrified look: They promoted you to Major Crimes?

Amy doesn't see it as a promotion. In fact, she sees it as punishment. And as she takes a seat at an empty desk, we CUT TO:

4. INT. VAN – DAY

Sammo wakes up and finds himself in the van. He has been unconscious for hours. He sits up quickly and discovers there's a SMALL ELECTRONIC DEVICE strapped to his chest. What the hell is it?

"It's a bomb," a voice says, reading his mind and ours.

Sammo looks up to see a MAN sitting in the driver's seat, safe behind an IRON SCREEN. It's the "cop" we saw before. The man introduces himself as DANIEL DARIUS and explains he saw Sammo on TV last night and was very, very impressed. He knew right then that Sammo is just the dogged investigator he needs to help him. Darius tells Sammo he just got out of prison after serving fifteen years for his part in stealing the $50 million McQueen Collection from Matheson's Auction House. He was the only one who got caught . . . the others got away. But that's about to change. Sammo is going to find them and get Darius his share, plus interest, in twelve hours.

The bomb is Darius's idea of "strong motivation." It can only be deactivated with a uniquely encrypted mini-disk. Any attempt to open the case, freeze it, break it, magnetize it, x-ray it, or any other tampering will set it off and create a blast capable of killing him and everyone around him. It also has a motion sensor. It will explode if Sammo doesn't keep moving, sort of a guarantee that Sammo won't sit still when he should be doing his job. As fair warning, the bomb will BEEP FOUR TIMES if Sammo is engaging in any behavior that will cause detonation. The fifth beep is KA-BLAMMO. Darius also advises Sammo to stay away from microwave ovens, bug zappers, and anyone with a pager. The bomb is still kind of buggy.

Darius tells Sammo he will find a CELL PHONE in his pocket, which Darius will use to contact Sammo periodically to check up on his progress, beginning with a call in forty minutes to brief Sammo and his team on the pertinent details of the robbery.

There's a CLICK as the van doors unlock. You are free to go, Darius says, the police station is about a mile away. Darius tells Sammo to hurry. Sammo hops out of the van.

5. EXT. ALLEY – DAY

The van speeds off, leaving Sammo alone in the alley. This has not been his day. He stands there for a moment, in shock, when THREE BEEPS from his bomb shake him out of it and he starts marching down the alley. He starts to make a call on the cell phone when SEVERAL STREET THUGS peel out of the shadows. They want the phone. He can't give it to them. They also want his wallet. He can't do that, either. In fact, he really can't stop at all. They don't like that answer. And as they whip out their weapons and move in for the kill, and his bomb starts to BEEP, we FADE OUT.

END OF ACT ONE

ACT TWO

1. EXT. ALLEY – DAY

Sammo has no choice, he has to fight. On the third beep, he does a flying kick, defending himself while also trying to keep the bomb from taking any hits. It isn't easy, but he prevails and marches on, leaving the street thugs groaning on the ground in his wake and vowing to get even someday.

2. INT. MCU – DAY

Terrell gets a call on his cell phone. It's Sammo, telling him to meet him in the parking lot right away . . . and to bring the bomb squad. Terrell, thoroughly confused, rushes downstairs, Grace and Amy right behind him.

3. EXT. POLICE STATION – PARKING LOT – DAY

Sammo is marching around the parking lot, ordering the officers around him to clear the area, when Terrell, Grace and Amy come out. What is going on, Terrell asks. Sammo explains his unique predicament and discovers that Amy is now part of the team. His cell phone rings. It's Darius.

Darius assumes the team is gathered around and tells them to feel free to ask questions. He recounts his tale, which we illustrate with cool flashback as Sammo keeps moving, and Cragg arrives with his BOMB SQUAD. We learn:

Darius is an explosives expert. He was recruited by phone by a mastermind he never met. A sizeable amount of money appeared in his bank account. He was told that was his just for taking the call. After completion of the robbery, three times as much money would be wired into offshore accounts that had been created. He was told he'd get a call sometime soon with instructions. Six months later, the call came. He was told to go to a warehouse. When he got there, there were four other people waiting. On a table, there were envelopes addressed to each of them with more money inside and specific instructions on their role in a robbery to be committed in the next 90 minutes. There were uniforms, a DWP van, and a map.

They drove the van to a specific manhole. They went down the sewer. All the equipment they needed was waiting for them in the tunnel. They broke into the auction house from below; it was Darius's job to blast the hole. It was delicate work; a mistake could set a fire inside the auction house or collapse the sewer tunnel on them.

Once the hole was made, it was up to a twenty-year-old woman to negotiate the laser beam security system with gymnastic skill and disable the alarm. A safecracker got into the vault while Darius and two others stole the paintings, jewels, etc. Meanwhile, they were in constant radio contact with a lookout man in the truck. They were only to steal specific items on the mastermind's list, but Darius couldn't resist pocketing a ruby he found.

They split up after the robbery, but later that same day Darius drove through an intersection and got hit by some jerk who ran a red light and got caught with the ruby on him. He went to jail; the others got away.

Darius gives them what little he knows about his mysterious cohorts. The driver had a UNIQUE TATTOO on his forearm. Darius reminds Sammo he only has eleven more hours . . . and hangs up.

Cragg isn't having an easy time studying the bomb, since he has to run alongside Sammo to do it, but it looks authentic to him. The only way to safely defuse it is by inserting the encrypted mini-disc. There's no way to replicate the disk without knowing what the encrypted data is.

Amy knows something about the McQueen robbery and knows that investigators were certain the "gymnastic" woman was a female thief named CELINE VASHON, but they could never prove it. Terrell says he'll pursue that lead—Amy and Grace have to track down the Tattoo guy.

Sammo says what about me? Terrell says you stay here, keep walking, we'll handle it. Sammo says no way; it's his life at stake here. Amy says you're a walking bomb, we can't let you endanger the lives of others. Terrell gets an idea. He commandeers Cragg's bomb disposal truck which, theoretically, should contain Sammo if he explodes. Sammo doesn't find that very reassuring.

4. EXT. MANSION – DAY

Crime pays. The bomb truck speeds up the long drive, coming to a screeching stop in front of a spectacular house. Terrell and Sammo get out. The truck doesn't handle like Terrell's boxster, but he drives it the same way. Which would be bad enough, but Sammo was also forced to pace around the truck the whole ride. So now Sammo is more than a little carsick. Clearly, this is going to be a long day.

They are about to knock at the door when Terrell spots CELINE working out in the yard, doing one incredible gymnastic move after another. Did you see Catherine Zeta-Jones in *Entrapment?* Well, this lady is even sexier when she moves—and she knows it—and is aware of the seductive effect it has on Terrell as he tries to question her about her life of crime. Sammo, meanwhile, is forced to keep moving, working up a sweat of his own while Terrell and Celine play their game of cat-and-mouse.

Celine doesn't deny that she's a thief, but she doesn't admit it, either. She talks of the theft of the McQueen Collection as one of the "Great Crimes of the Century" and admires its flawless execution. Whoever their mysterious employer was, he or she was rich and brilliant. Sammo and Terrell leave with nothing except the certainty that she was involved.

5. EXT. BAD SIDE OF TOWN – DAY

Amy is driving and Grace is in the passenger seat, frustrated. Sammo's life is literally ticking away, and Amy is driving like an senior citizen. Amy argues that charging through the street, siren wailing, tires screeching, not only ruins the car and endangers citizens, but could alert the people they are going to see that they are coming. Amy and Grace have used law enforcement databases to trace the TATTOO to an expert getaway driver, an ex-con named MALIK, whom we SEE in a PHOTO on Grace's lap. The tattoo is a sign of membership in an ultraviolent prison gang. They arrive at the gang's hangout. Grace advises Amy to let her handle this.

6. INT. GANG HANGOUT – DAY

If you are a woman, especially an attractive one, this is the last place you'd want to be, unless you were backed up by a heavily armed contingent of soldiers. The instant Grace and Amy step inside, they become meat. Or at least that's the look the DOZEN BRUTAL THUGS give them as they step inside. Malik is in the back of the room.

Grace is utterly at ease. Amy isn't, and is about to reach for her gun when Grace stops her and whispers, "That's not necessary. I can handle it. No matter what happens, you stay with Malik."

Grace identifies herself as a police officer and says they want Malik. They want her. And as they move in to take what they want, Grace strikes. In the melee, Malik bolts. Amy chases after him.

7. EXT. GANG HANGOUT – DAY

Malik jumps into a car and speeds off. Amy has to dive out of the way of the car, which fishtails into an intersection, narrowly avoiding the ACCIDENT he causes. Amy runs around the building to their car, only to find Grace already behind the wheel, demanding to know what took Amy so long.

8. EXT. STREETS – DAY

They charge after Malik, only to get caught in the gridlock caused by the accident he created. Amy opens her passenger door right in front of a speeding motorcycle, which has to brake to avoid hitting it. Amy commandeers the cycle and the helmet and gives chase. She drives the motorcycles along THE TOP OF A ROW OF PARKED CARS, flying off the last one and into the air, coming to a stop in front of Malik's SPEEDING CAR. She pulls out her gun, takes careful aim, and FIRES, blowing out his front tire. The car spins to a stop.

Grace comes running up just as Amy pulls Malik out of the car. Grace clearly underestimated Amy. Fact is, most people do.

"Read him his rights," Amy says, "I'll be right back."

"Where are you going?" an astonished Grace asks.

"To put my card under the wipers of every car I damaged," Amy says. "So the citizens can be properly reimbursed."

That's when we SHIFT PERSPECTIVES, and SEE the street scene from ABOVE, from

THE POV OF A SNIPER

on a rooftop. His CROSSHAIRS move from Amy to Grace to Malik and BANG!

BACK TO SCENE

Malik falls, DEAD. Grace spins around, her gun aimed at the rooftop, but the SNIPER is already gone. And on their surprise, we FADE OUT.

END OF ACT TWO

ACT THREE

1. INT. MCU – DAY

Amy discovers that the case files in the computer on the robbery of the McQueen Collection were "tagged"—calling them up activated a data chain, resulting in an e-mail being posted publicly in the alt.crime newsgroup on the Internet. It read simply: The box is open. Someone out there, probably the mastermind behind the robbery, wanted to know immediately if any one ever reopened the investigation. Now he's knocking off the perpetrators before Sammo can get to them. And if he succeeds, Sammo will die in just six hours.

2. INT. BOMB TRUCK – DAY
Sammo and Terrell get a call from Grace . . . someone else is on the same trail they are . . . Celine could be in grave danger. Terrell makes a big U-turn and heads back the way they came.

3. EXT. MANSION – DAY
Sammo and Terrell rush back. Celine is surprised to see them. Terrell warns her that she's in grave danger and has to come with them. Celine says that's a new approach—not very effective, but new. She's not going anywhere.

That's when THE SNIPER opens FIRE, just missing her.

Celine does an AMAZING SERIES of GYNMASTIC MOVES to avoid the bullets and take cover. Terrell takes cover and RETURNS FIRE. Sammo also takes cover, but the moment he does, his BOMB STARTS TO BEEP, forcing him to abandon his cover and become a moving target for the sniper. Sammo dodges the bullets, through some incredible agility and cleverness of his own, and the sniper flees.

Celine doesn't need any more convincing. She'll go with them and tell them whatever they need to know, as long as it falls short of implicating herself in the robbery, of course. She got paid in full for her role in the robbery and never really had any interest in who the mastermind was.

Sammo's phone rings. It's Darius. He wants a progress report. They plug the phone into the hands-free system so they can all talk to him. Celine introduces herself to Darius, and they compare notes. She has no idea who masterminded the robbery but, years later in Nice, she ran into one of the other participants on another job. His name is KANE. Where is he now, asks Terrell. South America,

Celine replies, he's become a missionary. The Nice job went bad, some people got killed, and it really affected Kane, who sought solace with Father Bosley, who converted him to a life of God.

Darius isn't surprised; if anyone could do it, it's Father Bosley, who went from prison to prison saving souls. Sammo realizes they've found two connections . . . all the felons are ex-cons and at least three of them knew Father Bosley. Terrell says it's time they have a few good words with him themselves. Darius says you better make it fast . . . you only have a few hours left. Terrell calls Grace and Amy and tells them to find Father Bosley.

4. INT. HALFWAY HOUSE – DAY

This is where ex-cons go between prison and their return to the streets. Grace and Amy run into a few familiar faces, but none of the ex-cons hold a grudge. They've all found peace and contentment, thanks to Father Bosley. Grace and Amy find Father Bosley and immediately confront him about his involvement in the auction house robbery. He claims to have no idea what they are talking about. He lives simply, he has no interest in material things, they can check that out themselves. And he certainly isn't going to help someone else find people to commit crimes, that would go against everything he's trying to accomplish here. Amy asks where Bosley gets the money to fund his activities. He says he gets grants from the state and local government, as well as generous donations from private parties. Grace wants to know who has access to his records. Bosley says the prison authorities and a few of his patrons who like to know the progress of his work. Amy wants a list of those patrons. He points them to a plaque on the wall. One name stands right out: Thomas McQueen.

5. EXT. McQUEEN'S ESTATE – DAY

Terrell and Sammo barge right past his security people and confront McQueen with what they know . . . and what they've guessed. Meanwhile, Celine helps herself to a tour of the place. McQueen is amused by their story, but says there isn't a shred of evidence in it. That's when Celine returns—she has something to show them. She leads them to a hidden room, which is filled with all the STOLEN ARTWORK. Terrell is impressed—they should bring a professional thief with them whenever they question somebody. McQueen was forced to auction off half his holdings in a messy divorce, but he couldn't bear to let the items go. So he picked his robbery team from Father Bosley's records, planned and staged the robbery, and kept the insurance settlement.

Why didn't you pay Darius his share, Sammo asks. Because, McQueen says, he broke the rules. He took that ruby. If he'd done as I told him, he wouldn't have gotten caught. It's his own fault. I don't pay for failure.

Sammo's cell phone rings. It's Darius. He tells Sammo to handcuff himself to McQueen, or he'll detonate the bomb right now. Sammo does, but doesn't understand how Darius knows where they are . . . and who they are with. There's a camera on the bomb, Darius says. He has seen and heard everything all along.

You've got your man, Sammo says. Deactivate the bomb.

I don't care about him, Darius says. I care about the money.

Darius wants McQueen to wire $50 million into Darius's offshore account within the two hours left on the bomb timer, or Sammo and McQueen, and anyone around them, will be blown to bits. And on this unsettling turn, we FADE OUT.

END OF ACT THREE

ACT FOUR

1. EXT. BANK – NIGHT

The bomb truck screeches to a stop outside. Terrell jumps out. There are no police officers to be seen. He's furious. He tells Sammo and McQueen to go into the bank—he'll start evacuating people from around the building. Terrell rushes off. As soon as he is out of their sight (and out of view of Darius's camera and mike), Terrell pulls out his cell phone and is patched in to Amy, who is in

2. A MOBILE COMMAND UNIT

On a street nearby, working at a computer. Grace is leaning over her shoulder. Amy is patched into the bank's computer system and is prepared to intercept and trace the wire. Terrell believes the camera on Sammo can't transmit very far. If Darius has watched their every move, he must be mobile and is probably nearby. Terrell tells Grace to have officers fan out in a one-mile radius and start looking for the van that Sammo described. Terrell will search on foot. Meanwhile, we see

3. THE STREET THUGS

Who attacked Sammo way back in Act One. They are bruised and bandaged, but they still look tough. One of them spots Sammo and McQueen heading for the bank. Isn't that the guy who kicked our butts?

Yes, it is. And it's time for payback.

The thugs pull out their weapons and advance on

4. EXT. BANK – NIGHT

Sammo and McQueen are heading into the bank. There's only a few minutes left on the timer, there is no time to waste. Which is not a good time to be surrounded by a dozen vicious thugs with a grudge. Sammo tries to tell them this is not a good time—he's handcuffed to a prisoner and he's got a bomb around his chest that's within minutes of exploding. But these violent morons aren't persuaded. They move in.

5. EXT. STREETS – NIGHT (VARIOUS SHOTS)

As Terrell and Grace run frantically through the streets, searching for the van. Time is running out. Grace spots the van. She yanks open the doors . . . to find a couple teenagers making out. False alarm. But the seconds are still ticking away.

6. EXT. BANK – NIGHT

Sammo takes on the bad guys, using the startled McQueen like a weapon, flinging his body around like a bat. He manages to prevail once again, but time is running out. They rush into the bank.

7. INT. BANK – NIGHT

Sammo shows his badge, shows his bomb, and tells everyone but the manager to evacuate the building. The manager hits the silent alarm. Sammo explains that this isn't a robbery, he's a police officer, but then gives up—why bother explaining? Who'd believe it? Sammo drags the manager to a computer terminal and tells McQueen to give him the information they need to make the transfer.

8. EXT. STREETS – NIGHT

Amy reports to Terrell that the transfer has begun. And there's only four minutes left on Sammo's timer. Terrell spots the van, parked on a busy overpass. He yanks open the rear doors and aims his gun inside. There is DARIUS, at a computer terminal, watching the video feed from the camera on Sammo. Terrell tells Darius to come out with his hands up.

Darius steps out of the van and raises his hands, flinging the mini-disc off the overpass in the same motion. Terrell watches in horror as the mini-disc sails into the L.A. River below.

You shouldn't have tried to stop me, Darius says. Now your friend will die. Terrell decks him. Grace rushes up to join them. Terrell tells her to arrest Darius. Where are you going, she asks. To defuse that bomb, Terrell says, running off.

9. INT. BANK – NIGHT

The transfer is complete. But the bomb is still ticking down. There's only two minutes left! Sammo takes out his handcuff key, uncuffs McQueen, and tells him and the manager get out—fast. McQueen and the manager run out of the bank, nearly colliding with Terrell as he rushes in.

Go, Sammo says, while there is still time.

Terrell waves Sammo off and tries to look casual. Relax, we caught Darius. Now I can disarm this little firecracker. Stand still. Sammo does. The bomb begins to beep.

Just ignore that, Terrell says, looking around for something. He finds a letter opener and jams it into the bomb.

Are you sure you know what you're doing, Sammo asks.

Of course I do, Terrell says. Not that it makes a difference with only twenty-nine seconds left and the bomb on its THIRD BEEP.

Terrell pries the bomb out of its casing, puts it on a table, and yanks out a MICROCHIP. The bomb stops beeping. "Disarmed," he says.

Sammo sags into a chair, relieved. "Why didn't you do that before?"

The BOMB starts to BEEP again. Terrell yanks Sammo out of the chair. "Because before I didn't have to pretend I knew anything about defusing bombs. RUN!"

They rush to the door.

10. EXT. BANK – NIGHT

Sammo and Terrell are barely out the door when the building EXPLODES behind them, vaulting them both into the air, a massive fireball rising into the night sky behind them.

Sammo looks up from the pavement at Terrell as bits of rubble rain down all around them. "You're insane."

"That's my best quality," Terrell says.

Sammo smiles: "I know." And we FADE OUT.

THE END

seaQuest 2032 Pitch/Leave-Behind ("Depths of Deceit")

Here is a typical leave-behind for an episode of *seaQuest 2032*.

SEAQUEST 2032
"Depths of Deceit"
Treatment

With Larry Deon nearly dead, lying on a hospital bed somewhere, there is a vacuum in power at Deon International. Alexander Bourne is mounting a hostile takeover.

Captain Hudson discovers that Bourne is mounting the takeover to gain control of *Barracuda*, a high-tech "stealth" sub that Deon has secretly been developing for years . . . a sub that's more powerful than *seaQuest*. With *Barracuda* in Macronesian hands, Bourne could conceivably regain dominance over the sea.

Hudson doesn't know how to battle proxies and stocks, but he knows someone who can—his father, Charles Hudson, a global entrepreneur and power broker whom Oliver hasn't talked to in two decades. A man who, incidentally, holds the largest share of Deon stock outside of Deon himself.

What we will discover is that Charles Hudson leaked the information about the *Barracuda* sub to Bourne, knowing that Bourne would mount a takeover and that Oliver would have to come to him for help, forcing a reconciliation Charles has sought for twenty years.

What Charles doesn't know is that Larry Deon is very much alive and very well—and that he is actively manipulating Charles,

Oliver, and Bourne to get rid of them all. Deon has formed a secret alliance with General Stassi, promising him *Barracuda*, which will give Stassi the military might he needs to overthrow Bourne and take control of Macronesia himself.

Deon also frames Charles Hudson, making it look like Charles sold the *Barracuda* information to Bourne, committing treason against the UEO, . . . and like Oliver was in on it. Charles is indicted, and Oliver is relieved of command of *seaQuest*. With *Barracuda* under his control, Stassi plans to destroy *seaQuest*, then mount a coup.

The Hudsons have to reconcile their differences and prevent both the destruction of *seaQuest* and a potential coup that could explode into global war.

Oliver and Charles take off in a shuttle, but are intercepted by *Barracuda*, which overwhelmingly outguns them. Using cunning and skill, they are able to elude *Barracuda* until *seaQuest* comes to their aid. Teaming with *seaQuest*, the Hudsons are able to destroy *Barracuda*.

Bourne remains in power, and Deon reclaims his company, but at least the world is at peace—and so are, after twenty years, Charles and Oliver Hudson.

seaQuest 2032 Beat Sheet ("Depths of Deceit")

Here is a typical beat sheet for an episode of *seaQuest 2032*. You'll notice it has a slightly different format than the other beat sheet. Showrunners have their own styles, which can be reflected in their beat sheets, too. You'll also notice some changes in the story between the leave-behind and the beat sheet, which is a normal part of the development process. The story changed again by the time the script was written. Alas, the script was among several that weren't filmed because the show got cancelled in midseason. Again, that isn't unusual and is part of doing business. The important thing is that you get paid whether the script is shot or not!

SEAQUEST 2032
"Depths of Deceit"
Rough Beat Sheet by
Lee Goldberg and William Rabkin

TEASE

EXT. SPACE – An unmanned Space Station blows a DRONE to smithereens with a plasma laser blast.

INT. DEON INTERNATIONAL BOARDROOM – We see this has been a demonstration of the Deon Platform, the space-based defense system Deon has been developing for the UEO. McGath is impressed. That's when he's told there has been a change in terms—now anyone can rent the protection of the Platform for $40 million a month. Who approved this? The new majority stockholder. The doors open to reveal the stockholder is ALEXANDER BOURNE.

ACT ONE

OCEAN – *seaQuest* gets in a skirmish protecting Deon employees, who are fleeing across the free zone from Macronesian troops who are "nationalizing" Deon's colonies. Hudson calls McGath to protest, learns about Bourne's control of Deon and space platform.

SEAQUEST – CAPT. BEAU WINDOM of the COBRA arrives to support *seaQuest* maintaining peace along the free zone. The *Cobra* was the flagship of the fleet until *seaQuest* reappeared and relegated Windom to non-player on the global-oceanic scene.

Lucas briefs Hudson on details of the Deon Platform. Hudson gives us his theory that Bourne is advancing along the free zone, and once he has Deon's space platform under his control, he will invade. Hudson wants to do something—but feels powerless. Then he has a realization. Hudson abruptly takes twenty-four-hour leave, puts Ford in command of operation, borrows a shuttle.

MACRONESIA – Stassi and Bourne talk. Stassi says there's unrest along the Free Zone that we can't quell. Macronesian dissidents say all money is going into the war machine, nothing is going to the people. Bourne says drop some nerve gas and that will quiet the dissidents. Stassi says one hundred thousand martyrs are not what we need . . . we have to stop this drive for conquest and solidify support. Bourne says soon it will all be over. Soon there will be nothing left to conquer because it will all be ours.

NEW ORLEANS – Hudson goes and sees his father, Charles, a global entrepreneur and powerbroker with whom Oliver hasn't spoken in years. Charles is a big stockholder at Deon. Will his father help Oliver stop Bourne?

ACT TWO

NEW ORLEANS – Charles is pleased that Hudson has come to him for help, his attitude has always been that as soon as Oliver "grew up," he'd see that Charles was right about way world worked. Charles agrees to help—his way. Oliver swallows his pride and thanks his father.

FREE ZONE – A dissident ship blows up a Macronesia ship, then flees across the Free Zone. *seaQuest* rescues the dissidents, but the *Cobra* breaks ranks and chases the Macronesians across the free zone and into Macronesian waters. Windom calls for *seaQuest* to join, but Ford refuses, forcing Windom to run back, his tail between his legs.

SOMEPLACE – Hudsons are there to meet someone. . . . Charles says to Oliver that whatever happens, don't interfere. This is my world you are in now, don't get in my way. A figure steps out of the shadows—it's STASSI. Seems he is the real leader of the dissidents.

Charles offers Stassi a deal: I'll back your overthrow of Alexander Bourne if you agree to return all Deon nationalized property and give up Macronesia's stake in Deon International. In return, I'll get you all the weapons and I'll make sure the UEO turns a blind eye to your internal strife. Oliver begins to object, but Charles cuts him off at knees. Stassi agrees to the deal.

SOMEPLACE – Hudson tears into his father for dealing with Stassi. Charles says in the real world, things aren't clean. That's why you went into the Navy, you wanted absolutes, you wanted to push buttons and blow up your problems. This is how it really works. Hudson has to return to *seaQuest* . . . things at the Free Zone heating up.

SOMEWHERE – Bourne uses the space platform to blow up dissident colony.

FREE ZONE – Windom is furious with Ford for not backing him up. Ford says our job here is to protect refugees once they enter the free zone, not to invade or fuel discord inside Macronesia. Windom sees this as the UEO's opportunity to topple Bourne . . . to do what Bush didn't do in Iraq back in the 1990s. Ford orders Windom to do what he is told.

DEON INTERNATIONAL – BOARD MEETING – Bourne is catching hell from McGath and Deon board for using the Deon Platform to massacre people. Bourne defends himself, he says it was an unfortunate accident. Even so, he has controlling interest and can do what he pleases. "I don't think so, Al," someone says. That's when LARRY DEON suddenly appears, alive and very well. Deon has evidence that Charles Hudson leaked information about the space platform to Bourne. The board is outraged. Charles is arrested for treason. Bourne is suspended from the board pending investigation. Deon pulls Bourne aside, claims no hard feelings, but Bourne is too smart to believe that.

ACT THREE

DEON HQ – Larry Deon meets with Stassi, who has proof of his meeting with the Hudsons. We learn that Larry Deon intends to throw the weight of Deon International and the space platform behind Stassi in return for his help in Deon's secret scheme, which, incidentally, is falling right into place. Soon, Deon's two biggest obstacles, Hudson and Bourne, will be out of the picture.

SEAQUEST – Charles warns Hudson via vidlink that they've been tricked, Larry Deon is alive. But it's too late . . . Ford marches in with orders from UEO to relieve Hudson of command and place him under arrest for treason. Windom is given command of *seaQuest* and the mission . . . and he decides the *seaQuest* is going to cross the free zone and support a dissident attack. Ford argues that will leave the free zone unprotected. Windom says unprotected from what? Besides, the *Cobra* is here.

UEO HQ – McGath and Oliver Hudson have confrontation. Hudson wants to know why he was arrested. We learn of Stassi's "proof," and Hudson learns his father leaked space platform information to Bourne.

Hudson wants to know why Deon is still free after all the crimes he has committed. McGath says there's no proof. Hudson says the real reason is the UEO needs Deon, its technology and deep pockets. McGath says the world is not black and white, there are complexities you can't understand. Hudson says, Funny, that's what my father says.

FREE ZONE – *seaQuest* goes across the border to assist dissidents. Only, it was a ploy. Once *seaQuest* is in Macronesia, Bourne launches an invasion across the free zone. The *Cobra* is DESTROYED. They've been tricked.

ACT FOUR

NEW ORLEANS – Charles powerbrokers their freedom. Oliver confronts his father. Oliver can't believe his father gave Bourne the information about the space platform, potentially tipping balance of world power. Charles says that balance tips hourly, and I've done it many times, usually at a profit. I did it this time to see my son, so you'd come back. So you'd need me. So you'd respect me. Oliver is furious. There is right and wrong, there are absolutes, maybe I don't know where the line is, but I know I won't cross it. You did. And now we have to clean it up before world is plunged into war. Oliver says we can do it my way . . . and yours.

DEON INTERNATIONAL – Stassi says now is the time to blow up the Presidential Palace, while Bourne is absorbed in his invasion. Deon says okay, hits a button. We see the Space Platform blow up the Presidential Palace.

SEAQUEST – The Macronesian fleet is pouring across the border, the battle begins. *seaQuest* is barely able to keep the enemy at bay. Meanwhile, Oliver Hudson pilots a subfighter to *seaQuest*, narrowly escaping destruction. He hands the schematics of the Space Platform to Lucas. Where did you get these? Hudson says, my father has deep pockets and owns the company that built it. You have five minutes to reprogram the Platform or we're dead. Windom, humiliated, concedes command to Hudson.

DEON INTERNATIONAL – Stassi pulls a gun on Deon and says: "I'm arresting you for the murder of President Bourne." That's when Stassi is shot—by Alexander Bourne, who walks into the room with Charles Hudson. Deon is more impressed than surprised. Charles figured out what Deon was doing and cut a deal with Bourne. Deon asks what the deal was. Charles says Bourne promised to back out of Deon and relinquish control of the space platform. But Bourne has changed his mind—and targets *seaQuest*. Bourne hits the bottom. The platform fires. . . .

SEAQUEST – Lucas sends a transmission to the platform. Suddenly the Macronesian Alliance ships are blowing up, struck by the space laser. Lucas has fooled the platform into believing the Macronesian ships are *seaQuest*.

DEON INTERNATIONAL – Bourne, to his horror, discovers the platform is destroying his ships. Oliver Hudson comes on the vidlink—tells Bourne there is only one way to stop his entire fleet from being destroyed: Destroy the platform. Reluctantly, Bourne hits the self-destruct and the platform explodes.

NEW ORLEANS – The Hudsons reach a reconciliation and will no longer be estranged—they both learned to respect one another. Windom is relegated to a freighter, Deon is still in business, Bourne is still in power. The fragile balance of power has been restored.

Diagnosis Murder Beat Sheet ("A Passion for Murder")

Here's the first-draft beat sheet of a produced episode of *Diagnosis Murder*.

DIAGNOSIS MURDER
"A Passion for Murder"
First Draft Beat Sheet by
Lee Goldberg and William Rabkin

TEASE

INT. COMMUNITY GENERAL – ER – DAY
TOD GRIMES, thirties, a confident, well-dressed man, winds his way through the ER. He's looking for Dr. Sloan. He's pointed in the direction of pathology when he passes the ER doors . . . just as a beautiful, but frantic woman (STEPHANIE HITCHER), twenties, comes in with DAVE CRANSTON, thirties, who has been hit by a car while crossing the street. Dave is in serious shape. Tod jumps on the case, heroically performing some sort of emergency procedure, before anyone can stop him. Jesse shoves Tod off the man, and is about to call security, when Mark intervenes . . . Tod is a doctor. In fact, he's our new Chief of Staff. And on Jesse's surprise, and Stephanie's awe, we FADE OUT.

END OF TEASE

ACT ONE

INT. COMMUNITY GENERAL – DAY

An informal cocktail party is being held to welcome Tod and his wife, KIM, to Community General. All our regulars are here. We learn that Tod served his residency here, under Mark's tutelage, and that Mark was instrumental in luring this rising star back from Boston to the hospital, much to Kim's displeasure. Her career as a lawyer was flourishing in Boston, and she's very ambivalent about having to uproot. In fact, she's late for a plane . . . she still has things to tie up back east. She leaves, insisting that Tod stay and enjoy the party while she takes a taxi to the airport. Mark assures Tod that Kim will adjust; moving is never easy.

INT. COMMUNITY GENERAL – DAVE'S ROOM – NEXT DAY

Jesse is handling Dave's case. We learn that Dave needed an emergency splenectomy (or something like that) and suffered some serious bruises and contusions—but otherwise he was very lucky. We learn that Dave and Stephanie are pharmaceutical salespeople and were having lunch at downtown hotel before the accident. He wasn't paying much attention as he was leaving the restaurant, stepped off the curb right in front of a car. Jesse asks if there are any family members Dave would like him to contact. Dave says no, I don't have anyone. All he's really interested in knowing is if Stephanie has been by to visit. A nurse comes in with a bag containing Dave's clothing and belongings, which were stripped off him for the operation. Jesse notices some family photos have slipped out of his wallet, showing Dave with what appears to be a wife and kids. And on Jesse's concern, we go to:

INT. COMMUNITY GENERAL – DAY

Norman is showing Tod around, letting the new chief know what's ahead on his calendar. First up is a meeting with the rep from Jennings Pharmaceuticals. The rep turns out to be Stephanie. She really admires the way Tod handled the emergency yesterday and she'd like to take him to lunch to show her appreciation. Tod agrees. Her attraction to him is undeniable, and we get a sense that he's not immune to her interest.

INT. COMMUNITY GENERAL – LOUNGE – DAY
Jesse tells Mark and Amanda that he's concerned about Dave, who is behaving suspiciously. Dave told Jesse he had no loved ones to notify of his injury, but Jesse saw family photos in his wallet. Jesse's youthful curiosity is piqued, so he did a routine check with Dave's insurance company, and discovered Dave is married with two kids, and they live here in town. So why not let them know he's in the hospital? Mark says Dave is here for a few days, maybe he'll open up to you. But beyond that, if it doesn't impact on his medical condition, it's none of our business. Amanda has to run, she's having lunch with an old friend at Le Guerre. Mark tells her not to be late for Tod's first staff meeting. The man is a stickler for punctuality.

INT. LE GUERRE RESTAURANT – DAY
Tod and Stephanie have lunch. The sparks are really flying between them . . . which isn't lost on Amanda, who happens to be eating at the same place.

INT. COMMUNITY GENERAL – DAY
The staff is gathered for Tod's meeting, but Tod is a no-show. Amanda tells Mark she saw Tod at lunch, and there was some real heat between Tod and the rep. Mark dismisses any hint that Tod might be unfaithful, chalks it up to Tod's aggressiveness and charisma. Tod was probably working his charm to get the hospital a better rate on drugs.

INT. STEPHANIE'S APARTMENT – DAY
Tod and Stephanie are making love. He realizes he's late for the staff meeting, but his efforts to leave are no match for her sensual charms. As he melts back into her arms, we FADE OUT.

END OF ACT ONE

ACT TWO

INT. TOD'S HOUSE – DAY

Tod is showing Mark the new home he and Kim have bought. It's a fixer-upper, and smaller than they'd like, but the price was right and it was near the hospital. As they enter the house, they are shocked to find Stephanie inside, unpacking the boxes and decorating. Tod, shocked, tells her to leave. She says she can't leave. Tod has no eye for decorating. Tod all but throws her out, then has to face Mark, whose harsh look betrays his disapproval of what he's seen. Mark asks Tod if he'd like to talk . . . not as co-workers, but as friends. Tod admits his tryst and shares his tremendous guilt. Tod tells Mark that his marriage has been rocky lately, but he doesn't want to lose Kim.

INT. COMMUNITY GENERAL – DAVE'S ROOM – DAY

Jesse comes in to find Dave on the phone with his company; apparently Dave has just been fired. Dave is shaken by the news and again asks Jesse why the nurses won't let Stephanie in to see him. Jesse says no one has been prevented from seeing him, anyone is welcome to visit Dave, including Dave's family. Dave says I don't have a family anymore. Dave says he can't believe Stephanie hasn't tried to see him—she must be around, she's handling the Community General account and negotiating the new supply contract for the year. Jesse says if he sees her, he'll tell her Dave would like her to stop by. Jesse leaves, more suspicious than ever.

INT. TOD'S HOUSE – DAY

Kim comes home, is unpacking, when Stephanie shows up. She tells Kim she's working with Tod, and would like to get him a special gift for giving her the Community General contract. Stephanie talks about Tod in a creepy, intimate sort of way that makes Kim very uncomfortable and that clearly implies that they are lovers. Stephanie sees that Kim isn't going to be much help and leaves, but not before complimenting Kim on her clothes and hairstyle and wondering aloud how they would work for her.

INT. COMMUNITY GENERAL – TOD'S OFFICE – DAY

Tod is meeting with Norman when the secretary buzzes—the rep from the pharmaceutical company is here to see you. Tod tells the secretary he is tied up all day. Secretary says the woman insists. Tod says tell her our business is concluded and hangs up. Norman asks if there is a problem. Tod says no. Norman smiles, assuming Tod is just being a tough negotiator. That's when the door bursts open and Stephanie marches in, though at first we can be forgiven for not recognizing her. Because now she looks *just like Kim*, she's got the same hairstyle and clothes. She smiles at Tod, who is too shocked—make that too horrified—to say a word.

Norman says it was time for a break anyway and leaves them alone (but not before whispering to Tod that "every penny counts.") Once they're alone, Stephanie goes to Tod, who stays the hell away from her. She doesn't take that well. She says I love you, Tod. I want you.

Tod tells her that he loves his wife, and what they did the other day was a terrible mistake. Stephanie doesn't believe that. Tod says, as carefully as he can, that it might be a good idea if Stephanie got some help. She says Tod can give her all the help she needs. Tod tells her that under the circumstances, he would prefer to deal with someone else from her company and that he doesn't want to see her again.

INT. COMMUNITY GENERAL – OUTSIDE TOM'S OFFICE – DAY

Stephanie storms out and bumps into Jesse, who tells her about Dave's condition and suggests that Dave would really like to see her. This only seems to piss Stephanie off more. She says she'll see Dave on her way out.

INT. COMMUNITY GENERAL – DAVE'S ROOM – DAY

The moment Stephanie walks in, Dave's face lights up. He is so glad to see her. And he loves her sexy new look. It's not for you, Stephanie says coldly. Dave is confused, doesn't understand what she's talking about. She says I wish you had died. Dave isn't getting this at all. He tells her he loves her, that he's been longing to see her. She says get over it—the relationship is over.

He says it can't be, I gave up my wife for you, my family for you. She doesn't care. She's found someone else. Dave wants to know who. She says it's Dr. Tod Grimes, but if it wasn't Tod, it would have been someone else.

Dave implores her to give him another chance. She says I'm going to Tod's house tonight, giving myself to him with all my body and soul, and you will already be forgotten. On her way out, she tells Dave how sorry she is that he lost his job. Dave asks how she knew. She says someone had to tell them how you were slipping—your poor sales figures were dragging us all down—I had no idea that they'd actually give me your office. Oh well, that's life. And after that final stab, she leaves Dave, a wrecked man.

INT. COMMUNITY GENERAL – LOBBY – DAY
Stephanie goes to the elevator, just as it opens and Kim steps out. Kim is stunned to see Stephanie here—and looking just like her. Stephanie only smiles, says she loves the way Tod giggles when you lick his ear, and gets into the elevator. Kim marches down the corridor in a fury.

INT. COMMUNITY GENERAL – CORRIDOR – DAY
Tod and Mark are walking down the hall. Tod is telling Mark that he thinks Stephanie is a nut, perhaps obsessed, and wonders what he can do about her. Mark says maybe Steve can be of some help. They are discussing possible approaches when a furious Kim confronts Tod, rips him apart for his wild affair. She creates an enormous scene, almost like a grenade going off. She says she's going back to Boston on the next plane. Kim storms out. And on everyone's shock, we cut to:

INT. TOD'S HOUSE – NIGHT
Tod is pleading his case to Kim. He knows what he did was wrong, and that Kim may never forgive him. But their marriage is too important

to just throw away. He pleads with her to work it out with him. She goes into a violent tirade. He backs off, says he will be at the hotel if she wants to talk. He leaves. She stays behind, cries, starts breaking things. Suddenly, she's CUT DOWN by TWO GUNSHOTS through the window. And on her dead body, we FADE OUT.

END OF ACT TWO

ACT THREE

INT. TOD'S HOUSE – DAY
It's a crime scene. Mark and Steve are there. Looks like Kim was shot with a gun by someone standing just outside the window. Neighbors report hearing a loud argument shortly beforehand. Tod is convinced Stephanie killed his wife. Steve will look into it.

INT. STEPHANIE'S HOUSE – DAY
Steve meets with her. She admits to the affair, but claims it was Tod who was obsessed with *her*. Says Tod's big worry was his wife finding out about them. Steve asks her where she was last night. She says she was having a business dinner. Steve asks with whom. She says Norman Briggs.

INT. COMMUNITY GENERAL – DAY
Jesse is examining Dave's chart. He's very worried about test results taken last night—his blood pressure, heart rate, and other levels are unusually high. Jesse is worried about complications. He goes to see Dave, who has heard about what happened to Tod. Dave decides Jesse has to know the truth: Dave was having an affair with Stephanie. She is a sexual predator. Dave lost everything for her, and when he had nothing more to give her, well, she pushed him in front of the car. Jesse is shocked. Dave says Stephanie is a very dangerous woman . . . and I'm not the first man she's sunk her fangs into.

INT. COMMUNITY GENERAL – DAY
Mark is stunned to see Tod there. Tod says where else could I go?

Mark says he can stay at the beach house, but Tod would rather work. Norman sees Tod and asks if he can have a word with him when he gets a chance. Tod says now is good for me. Norman invites Tod to his office. . . .

INT. COMMUNITY GENERAL – ELSEWHERE – DAY
Stephanie is supervising delivery of drugs or other business when Steve tracks her down. He tells her he discovered she has a license to carry a gun. She says she carries around a lot of drugs and she, as well as all the salespeople, are armed for their own protection. Steve would like to see the gun. Stephanie says he'll have to go to Pittsburgh. She left the gun with her mother . . . she hates to carry it and prefers her mother have it around to protect herself.

INT. COMMUNITY GENERAL – NORMAN'S OFFICE – DAY
Norman politely suggests that Tod take a few weeks off to get his life in order. Tod says but I just started here, I'd rather not. Norman says it really is for the best. Tod refuses and implies that Norman is really firing him. Norman reluctantly concedes the board would like to reexamine the whole situation. Tod keeps pushing, forcing Norman to say that the board is embarrassed, that after only a few days in town, Tod has already created a scandal. Perhaps it will die down in a few weeks, Norman says, and everything will be fine. Tod says screw the job and walks out, right into

INT. COMMUNITY GENERAL – CORRIDOR – DAY
Where Stephanie is. Tod throws himself at her, accusing her of killing his wife, taking his job, and is about to throttle her when Steve pulls him off. Tod takes a swing at Steve, who is forced to deck him and cuff him. Tod is under arrest. Norman shares a grim look with Mark—I think we're in the market for a new Chief of Staff.

END OF ACT THREE

ACT FOUR

INT. JAIL – DAY

Mark visits Tod, who tells Mark his life is over. He's lost everything—his wife, his job, his reputation, all because of one lapse. Mark says if Stephanie killed Kim, he'll prove it.

INT. COMMUNITY GENERAL – DAY

Jesse catches up with Mark, wants a medical consult on Dave. He shows Mark the perplexing test results and tells Mark what Dave told him about Stephanie. Mark says that's the second time today I've heard that story. Jesse says what do you mean? Steve comes up, says he has bad news. Steve talked to Stephanie's neighbors to see if any of them saw her leave her house at the time of the killing. Instead, a neighbor of Stephanie's has confirmed her alibi. Seems the neighbor is a peeping Tom, and Stephanie likes to parade around naked with the drapes open. She was definitely home when she said she was. Something clicks for Mark. He asks to see Dave's chart again . . .

INT. JAIL – DAY

Tod is bailed out . . . by Stephanie. She says she knows that Tod didn't mean the things he said . . . that he really wants her. Tod says you're right. She says now that Kim is gone, we can be together. Let's go home. Tod agrees. (A police officer overhears this.)

INT. COMMUNITY GENERAL – DAVE'S ROOM – DAY

Mark goes to see Dave, tells him he's concerned about the test results. They aren't consistent with a man who has been lying in bed after a splenectomy but of a man who's been under physical duress. Dave doesn't understand, what's physically stressful about lying here? Mark says nothing at all, which is the problem. But the results would make sense if you did something physically active like, say, going to Tod's house, killing his wife, and coming back here before your tests. Dave says Mark is nuts. Mark says you're a drug salesman like

Stephanie, I bet you have a gun license, too. You told Jesse your story to point a finger at Stephanie, but actually pointed it at yourself.

Dave breaks down—it's true, he killed Kim. But he meant to kill Stephanie. He saw what Stephanie was doing to Tod and knew she had to be stopped before she did to Tod what she did to him. When he saw the woman tearing up Tod's house, he assumed it was Stephanie. We all heard Kim say she was taking the next flight back to Boston.

Dave feels incredible remorse—all he wanted to do was save Tod, and instead he ruined him. The truth is, Dave stepped in front of the car . . . to kill himself.

Steve comes in. He just found out that Tod was bailed out of jail by Stephanie. Mark says we have to find them. Steve says a policeman heard them say something about going home.

INT. TOD'S HOUSE – DAY
Tod is letting himself be seduced by Stephanie. He's kissing her, holding her face, letting his hands slide down to her throat, and then he starts to squeeze. She tries to fight him off, but he only squeezes her throat tighter. He's going to kill her for what she's done . . . when Mark and Steve come in. Mark tells him that Stephanie didn't kill Kim, that Dave did. Tod says it's still Stephanie's fault; she drove Dave to it. Mark says if he kills her, she's won, she will have truly taken everything from him. Tod relents, releasing Stephanie, who is terrified.

INT. COMMUNITY GENERAL – DAY
It's a long time later. We learn that Mark and Tod have testified on Dave's behalf for a lenient sentence. Stephanie couldn't be prosecuted for any crime, but her deeds have caught up with her. After Tod's attack, she suffered a complete nervous breakdown and has been committed. Tod, meanwhile, is thinking about opening a general practice in some small town somewhere. Our heroes ponder the consequences one mistake can have on so many lives . . . and we fade out.

THE END

Diagnosis Murder Beat Sheet ("The Last Laugh")

Here is a beat sheet for a two-hour episode of *Diagnosis Murder*. You'll notice there is a major cliffhanger between the first and second hour. The cliffhanger is essentially a bigger version of the usual second-act break in a one-hour episode. In many ways, it serves the same function as a second-act break, only on a larger scale. The cliffhanger between the two hours of the show serves two functions: to make sure viewers stick around for the second half of the episode . . . and to create a strong break that would bring the viewers back the following *week* if the two-hour episode were broken into two one-hour episodes for syndication.

DIAGNOSIS MURDER
"The Last Laugh"
Rough Beat Sheet – First Draft
Written by
Lee Goldberg and William Rabkin

1. HOSPITAL – DAY
A bunch of surfers come into the hospital; they've been tossed around by the big waves. In the midst of dealing with all these surfer dudes, our heroes are talking about the big medical convention in Marina Del Rey, where Mark's friend DR. ELIOTT CRAIG, plastic surgeon to the stars, is going to be honored as Surgeon of the Year (Mark is delivering the award). Mark loves to needle Craig, who has

always been a tightass. In medical school, he was forever playing practical jokes on Craig to get him to crack a smile.

Jack is looking forward to the convention because EVE LURIE, twenties, his old med school flame, is going to be there. She was the first great love of his life. She left him because he wasn't "responsible." He's going to show her just how responsible he's become.

Amanda, meanwhile, is reuniting with some old friends, too, taking them out to an expensive dinner. They were all rich kids, and formed something of a clique. She's going to be a grand hostess while they are in her city.

2. HOTEL – CONVENTION – DAY

Mark arrives for a cocktail party honoring DR. ELIOTT CRAIG, the pompous "Michaelangelo of Flesh." He makes some disparaging remarks about his daughter Rita, who gave up medical school for a career in holistic medicine, which Craig views as one step removed from being a witch doctor. We meet also meet BONNIE, thirties, Craig's second wife and a former game show model, who wishes her husband would go easier on Rita, his daughter from his first marraige. Bonnie is wearing a DISTINCTIVE RED JACKET. We learn that she and Craig have taken a room at the hotel since they will be spending so much time there. We also meet LLOYD LARGO, thirties, a slick plastic surgeon who accuses Craig of stealing his patients. Jack and Lloyd know each other, and there is no love lost between them. And we meet Craig's nurse, KIMI MADISON, twenties, who is the ideal most women strive for when they have plastic surgery. Craig leaves the party; he has a meeting at his clinic.

3. HOTEL – POOL – DAY

Jack comes out, looking unusually conservative in a jacket and tie, and scans poolside, immediately spotting a drop-dead gorgeous woman in a string bikini. This is EVE, just arrived from back east (she couldn't wait to get her clothes off and get a little sun on her skin). She's surprised to see Jack—especially looking so "responsible." He asks her to dinner, and after some hedging, she agrees.

4. HOTEL – RESTAURANT – NIGHT

No expense is spared. Amanda and her friends are in a private room, eating and drinking and enjoying a private band. When the bill comes, Amanda grandly whips out a credit card. The waiter returns, the credit card is snipped in half. She gives him another. That one comes back snipped. She asks if they take checks. Not yours, he says. Everyone ends up having to chip in. Amanda is humiliated. She runs into Jack and Eve as she's leaving. After Amanda's gone, Jack picks up half her credit card from the floor. Hmmm.

5. CRAIG'S OFFICE – DAY

Dr. Craig is at his clinic early. He scans a photograph of a PATIENT into the computer, then sits down in front of the screen. He uses the computer to MORPH the face with a new nose, slight adjustment of eyes, etc. (We notice his desk has cut roses in a flowerpot.) While he does this, SOMEONE outside in the rosebushes opens a canister of nitrous oxide, which feeds into the air conditioner. Craig begins to giggle to himself, making outrageous changes to the Patient's body and face on the computer, laughing himself silly. But soon his laughter becomes more extreme, he's suffocating . . . he's laughing himself to death.

ACT TWO

6. HOSPITAL – DAY

Amanda is informed by Delores that her car is being towed. Amanda runs outside and is told her last two car payments bounced, so they are repossessing the car. They are towing it away as Jack drives up. He asks what's wrong, she says nothing, just a little car trouble. Jack says that's what you get for buying an expensive car. Never have a problem with mine. So, he asks, how was dinner last night. She marches off in a huff. He looks after her, curious.

7. HOSPITAL – DAY

Bonnie comes in to see Mark, who is just finishing up with yet another surfer dude. The seasonal high tide is bringing all the surf enthusiasts to the beach and wiping them out. Bonnie was also at the beach. In fact, she's complaining about a bad skin rash that suddenly appeared while she was walking along the shore. Mark asks her if she put on any sunscreen. She says yes, she gets so little sun. He guesses it was a common allergic reaction, and gives her a shot of cortizone. Mark is paged. He leaves Bonnie for a moment and gets the phone. It's Steve, with some bad news . . .

8. CRAIG'S OFFICE – DAY

Bonnie is comforted by her stepdaughter RITA, twenties. Mark talks to Steve, who says the nitrous oxide came from Craig's own office. Nurse Kimi says the canister, which they use for minor operations, was in the operating room yesterday afternoon, so it had to have been taken and placed out here sometime last night. They also found a bit of fabric in the thorny rosebushes. Mark says it's the same red as a jacket Bonnie wore last night. Steve turns to Mark, asks him to poke around, since this is Mark's world and not his own. Mark gladly agrees. Steve asks Mark to meet him at Craig's house later this afternoon.

9. HOSPITAL – DAY

Jack is on top of the world. His dinner with Eve went great last night. He really impressed her with how responsible he is. Responsible car. Responsible apartment. Responsible kisser. Mark asks Jack to poke around the convention, see what he can find out about Craig. Jack says I'll start by poking around his room at the hotel. Mark asks where Amanda is; Delores says she had to handle some personal business.

10. CRAIG HOUSE – DAY

Mark and Steve show up and ask Bonnie if she feels up for a few questions. Steve asks where her red jacket is, and she says it's hanging in my closet, you're welcome to take a look. He sends an officer up to look for it, then asks her some more questions. Where were you this morning, at the time of the murder? She says she was taking a walk on the beach, as Mark knows. Anyone see you? She says she took a picture for some tourist. Do you know where I can find him? She says no, all I remember was that he had an expensive camera and wore a jersey that didn't fit him. She adds that sunscreen gave her a rash, so she went to see Mark. Unfortunately, that is not an alibi. That's when the officer returns with news that there is no red jacket upstairs. Mark leaves the house, notices a gardener trimming juniper hedge. We notice there are no roses on the property.

11. HOTEL – DAY

Mark goes up to Lloyd's room. Lloyd opens the door, thinking it's room service, and Mark intrudes. Lloyd tries to shoo him out of room. It's common knowledge that Lloyd hated Craig. Lloyd says professional rivalry, that's all. Mark asks what he was doing this morning? That's when RITA CRAIG walks out of his bathroom in a bathrobe and says he was screwing my brains out, that's what.

Rita tells Mark she knows how it must look—like she was sleeping with Lloyd just to piss her father off. Fact is, she and her father haven't got along since she decided to drop out of medical school and explore holistic medicine. She says her father had no regard for other people's feelings. He never once set foot in her holistic health store in Venice. She had to borrow money to open it from Bonnie. Sweet lady my father used like some kind of glob of clay, practicing his plastic surgery techniques. We get backstory about Bonnie.

12. KILLEBREW'S OFFICE– DAY

Amanda confronts Killebrew, her trust fund manager, about her credit cards and her car (first she has him pay off her cab driver, since she has no cash—her automated teller machine ate her card). He shrugs it off as an unfortunate computer misshap that won't happen again. The person responsible has been fired. We learn he is an avid collector of an artist called Darabont, and owns two pieces of a three-piece set. He counsels Amanda to relax, her car will be back in her garage tomorrow and her credit cards are in the mail. She feels much better. Would he, ah, mind dropping her off at the hospital?

13. HOTEL ROOM – NIGHT

Jack breaks into Craig's room at the hotel and walks in on Lloyd and Nurse Kimi (Kimi figured why let a good hotel room go to waste?).

Lloyd decks Jack, then tumbles into the hall, followed by a nearly naked Kimi, just as Eve comes out of elevator. It's a mess. ("I see you haven't changed," Eve says, or something like that). Eve runs off. Lloyd wants an explanation, and so does Jack. It turns out Lloyd was also screwing Nurse Kimi (he will do anything to get back at Dr. Craig, short of murder). Kimi was also having an affair with Dr. Craig, who prefered "natural" beauty to his wife, whom he referred to as his "Frankenstein" monster. Did Bonnie know about the affair? Sure, she found Kimi and Craig together a few weeks ago.

14. HOSPITAL – NEXT DAY

Jack reports what he knows to Mark. Steve shows up, and Jack makes a crack about Steve's floral tie. Steve tells Mark that a witness saw a "woman in a red jacket" leaving Craig's office last night. Steve also tells Mark that Craig had talked to his lawyer about divorce and amending his will. He died before he got around to it. Now Bonnie gets $5 million. Mark takes a closer look at Steve's tie. Steve begs him not to make another crack. The tie came from a girlfriend and . . .

Mark picks up the phone. Steve asks what he's doing. Jack says he's calling the fashion police. Mark says I'm ordering flowers.

15. CRAIG'S HOUSE

Mark is asking her questions. Doorbell rings. Flowers arrive for Dr. Craig, congratulating him. Obviously, someone who didn't know he was dead. She takes them to the flowerpot. She starts to itch. Mark pulls up her sleeve. Hives. You didn't get a rash from the sunscreen— you got it from the roses. You're allergic to them—that's why there are no roses on the property, only at his office. She says that's ridiculous. There's a knock at the door; it's Steve with two uniformed officers. You're under arrest. But I'm innocent, she proclaims. Yeah, right. Brilliant Mark Sloan has done it again. The congratulatory flowers were for himself.

ACT THREE

16. COURTROOM – DAY

Rita, on the stand, admits she and her father had a rough time, and that she needed money. Didn't you ask to borrow money? Didn't he say no? She admits this. The defense attorney insinuates she has no money problems now, and with Bonnie in jail, will get all of it. Mark is on the stand and his testimony about flowers and sunscreen is a killer. Afterwards, Steve thanks his father for his help and says there's talk of getting a promotion out of this for speedy wrap-up.

17. HOTEL – DAY
Jack and Eve meet, he explains to her what happened in the hotel hall. He may have looked irresponsible when, in fact, he was being very responsible and was instrumental in solving the crime. She accepts his explanation, and they agree to go out again the following night.

18. HOSPITAL – DAY
Mark gets a call from Bonnie. She wants to see him. Meanwhile, Norman asks to see Amanda. Norman tells Amanda that her landlord has garnished her wages. She is shocked. Norman asks if there is anything he can do? Yes, I want to borrow your car for an hour.

19. JAIL – DAY
Mark and Bonnie meet. She pleads with Mark to help her. She is innocent. It was sunscreen. Her only alibi is the tourist. But how to find him? She gives him some description, the same she gave the police and her attorney. A guy with expensive running shoes and a fancy electronic camera had me take a picture of him, then he had it automatically take one of us together—he recognized me from my days on *The Price Is Right* (or whatever the game show is called). He wore a red jersey with the yellow #11 on it, but it was too small for him, and it was in bad shape.

Can Mark at least look into it for her? What possible harm could it do? Mark says he'll think about it.

20. AMANDA'S HOUSE – DAY
She arrives to find the landlord is moving her stuff out, under authority of the bailiff of the court. Her trust fund manager hasn't paid rent

in months, despite numerous warnings. So the landlord got a court judgment against her . . . she's out and she's furious. And she has nowhere to go.

21. HOSPITAL – DAY

Mark and Jack are discussing the tourist. Mark does some deductions: The tourist was wearing a rotten jersey that was too small for him. Yet he had very expensive shoes and camera, which means he's not poor, so that's not why he's wearing a jersey that's too small, which means the jersey has meaning. And why else would he be wearing an uncomfortable garment if not to share that meaning with others who might understand?

Jack guesses: You think he was going to a reunion. Perhaps even at a nearby hotel that afternoon—or why else would he be wearing the jersey on the beach that morning? Jack will check it out.

Steve barges in, confronts his father. He's heard Mark visited Bonnie in jail. Mark says he's helping her find the tourist. Steve is furious. How can he do this? Jeopardizing case, it's a blatant ploy to compromise the DA's best witness against her. Mark says what if she's innocent? Steve says you proved she's not. Mark says it's a circumstantial case. Steve says see, she already has you doubting. It's starting already. Steve says you could be letting a guilty woman out and causing me terrible professional embarrassment. Mark says it's something he has to do.

22. BEACHFRONT HOTEL – DAY

Jack is on his fifth hotel, goes into some scam about being sad about having missed the reunion. Turns out their colors are red and yellow. He looks up #11 in a yearbook and gets a name: DAVE McDON-NELL. He asks the hostess if she knows where he can find his old friend these days. Sure, he's returned to Seattle. Jack calls Mark, who tells him to take the next flight up.

23. KILLEBREW'S OFFICE – DAY

Amanda shows up at Killebrew's office. It's empty. Everything is gone. Amanda is horrified.

ACT FOUR

24. SEATTLE – DAY

Jack finds the tourist, Dave McDonnell. He has photos, not only of himself, but one he took of himself with Bonnie. This proves her alibi. Jack asks if he'd like an all-expense paid trip back to Los Angeles. That's when Jack realizes he stood up Eve. Damn!

25. TRIAL – NEXT DAY

The jury is about to return with their verdict. Mark runs in, interrupts everything. He has evidence. He drags in the tourist, the photos, everything. The judge drops all charges against Bonnie. The DA gives Steve a withering look, dresses him down for gross incompetence. Bonnie gives Mark a big hug. She's so grateful.

26. HOSPITAL – DAY

Jack comes into the doctor's lounge. It looks like Amanda has moved in. She says she's staying there for a night or two while they do some work on her condo. Besides, she is taking some long shifts, she'll be spending her nights here anyway. She puts up a brave front, but finally she breaks down and tells him everything. She says we'll never find him. Killebrew is probably out there spending my trust fund on another Darabont painting. Jack suddenly smiles. Don't worry, he says, we won't have to find him. He'll come to us.

27. ELSEWHERE IN HOSPITAL

Mark is on call. There's an accident at the beach. The surfer dudes are back, having been knocked around again by the fearsome high tide. Mark comes to a sudden realization. He rushes back to the office and looks at the photo. It's low tide. It should have been HIGH TIDE. Oh my god . . . she was guilty.

ACT FIVE

28. CRAIG HOUSE – DAY

Mark and Bonnie meet. Bonnie is sunning herself, slapping on that sunscreen. She readily admits to murdering her husband and thanks Mark for all his help. Mark vows to make sure she never sees a dime of the insurance money. He may not be able to send her to prison for murder, but he will do everything he can to gather enough evidence for the insurance company to prevail in a civil action. Mark finds his way out through the house, stumbles into the kitchen, where Dave McDonnell is making himself a veggie/protein shake. He thanks Mark for the free ticket to LA. Mark storms out.

29. HOTEL
Jack finds Lloyd Largo flirting with Eve. Jack chases Lloyd away, then apologizes to Eve and tries to explain why he inadvertently stood her up. This is his third strike. One more and they are finished. She's trying hard to believe he's changed, but Jack isn't making it easy.

30. HOSPITAL – DAY
Jack tells Amanda that the third painting in the Darabont trio (the one Killebrew doesn't have) was stolen from the Boston Museum two years ago and has not surfaced. Well, it just has. He shows her the painting. She says where did you get this? Jack says he had a "friend of the family" forge it. He also put the word out that he was the thief, and that he was willing to sell the painting for the right price, and that he could be reached at the hotel. She says what makes you think Killebrew will get the word? Jack says, he will.

31. POLICE STATION – DAY
Mark tells Steve that Bonnie is guilty. Steve says make up your mind, not that it matters anymore. He's been officially reprimanded for arresting Bonnie, but he thinks he's at least partially made up for it by finding the real killer: Rita, Craig's daughter.

Steve has just arrested Rita. He found Bonnie's red coat at Rita's house. Her alibi was a fraud. She had told Mark that she was with Lloyd Largo, giving them both an alibi at the same time. Turns out, she has none—she was alone. Lloyd went along with her because he was with a famous married actress that morning.

Mark says you are making a terrible mistake—she's innocent. Steve says the mistake I made was listening to you the first time. And on Mark's angst, we go to . . .

32. HOTEL

Jack arrives in a limo with Amanda. He checks in under the pseudonym JASON MILES and his assistant EUNICE (she elbows him). As soon as he walks through the lobby, he's noticed by two men, who we will come to know as DICKERSON and MAYER. Jack goes to the elevator. Before the door closes, a man steps inside. His name is CHARLES LANE, a representative of an interested third party who would like to buy the Darabont. Jack doesn't deal with middlemen. Tell your third party I have to meet face-to-face. Jack gets to his room, closes door in Lane's face, and then immediately catches hell from Amanda for being given a drab phony name. Jack reiterates how uncomfortable he is having her along on this—if Killebrew sees her, the con is ruined. She says I won't be seen. Besides, he would never figure me for a con like this. They go into another room. Jack opens the closet and a MAN steps out, holding a gun.

ACT SIX

33. PENTHOUSE – DAY

The gunman calls himself "JOHN SMITH." Fact is, he's the real thief who stole the Darabont, and wants to know what the hell Jack thinks he's doing horning in on his action. Jack says look, I'm doing you a favor. I line up the buyer, you sell the painting. I get a 50 percent cut. Smith cocks the trigger. Jack says okay, 25 percent—but you have to deliver the real painting. Smith goes to door, promising to keep his eye on Jack.

34. JAIL – DAY

Mark visits Rita. Mark learns that she was indeed the woman who visited Craig the night before he was killed. She asked to borrow money, but he refused. Mark tells her that Bonnie committed the murder, admitted it to him, and that he will do everything he can to get Rita freed. Rita says you can start by having Bonnie arrested. Mark explains double jeopardy, and if he can't get Bonnie for murder, the least he can do is amass enough evidence that the insurance company can press a civil action and never give her a dime. He vows to get Rita released somehow.

35. HOTEL – DAY

Jack calls Eve, tells her to meet him downstairs, he's rented a limo for a day of sightseeing. He meets her in the lobby. They are on the way to the car, when Dickerson and Mayer, the two who were watching Jack in the lobby, pull him aside and and throw him against the wall. You're under arrest. FBI. Eve storms off.

36. HOSPITAL – DAY

An orderly, clearly tourist DAVE McDONNELL in disguise, comes up to a nurse and tells her that Dr. Sloan is needed in operating room seven immediately. She pages Sloan. Mark, hearing the page, goes to the operating room. No sooner is he inside than he starts to giggle. He goes to the door; it's locked. He looks out the observation window, and there is Dave, waving good-bye to him. Sloan waves back, laughing. Mark finds the nitrous oxide—but the valve comes off in his hand. And on Sloan laughing, we FADE OUT.

ACT SEVEN

37. HOSPITAL – DAY

Mark is so overcome by the laughing gas, he is doing all kinds of schtick. Norman sees Mark through observation glass and breaks it down (throws a chair through it). Norman was on his way to chew out Mark for using an operating room without booking it first. For once, Norman's nitpickiness has actually made Mark's life better . . . by saving it!

38. PENTHOUSE

Jack explains to FBI agents what he is trying to do. They know about his crime family past, and about the forgery he's had made up, and they don't entirely believe him. There is a knock at the door. He peeks through hole. It's Eve. He begs FBI men to hide in closet. They do. Eve storms in, furious that she's been taken in by him again. Jack begs her to understand. The FBI agent thing was a practical joke. There's someone coming in the vent. Jack sticks Eve in the bathroom. The intruder is the thief. He wants to know what's going on. There's a knock at the door. Jack peeks out hole. It's Charles Lane, the middleman. Jack sticks the thief under the bed. Lane comes in and says the buyer will be here tonight. The picture better be here, too, or you'll pay dearly for the inconvenience. He leaves. Eve storms out of bathroom, slaps him, and leaves. The thief climbs back into the vent, says Jack has done good, the painting will be here. The FBI agents come out of the closet. We're going to be there, too.

39. CRAIG'S HOUSE
Mark goes to see tourist Dave McDonnell. But Bonnie says Dave has already left for the Caribbean to warm a chaise longue for me. Mark says he tried to kill me. She says what a shame. Mark says I think Dave planted the red jacket in Rita's apartment and framed her for the crime. Bonnie would love to stand around and talk, but she has packing to do. She's going to the Caribbean for a few months to work on her tan . . . right after Mark presents her with Dr. Craig's belated posthumous Surgeon of the Year award tonight at the closing of the convention. Mark leaves as the city trash truck comes up. He notices the jersey is in Bonnie's trash can. He takes the jersey, and amidst the other trash notices empty packets of Dave McDonnell's vitadrink mix. He swipes those, too.

40. HOSPITAL – DAY
Mark meets with Steve and tells him he's convinced Bonnie killed the tourist. Steve says just because she threw out his jersey? Mark says he did keep it all these years. Amanda comes back with tests Mark asked for—the vitapackets Mark dug out of the trash contained traces of rat poison. Steve says it's still just a guess, you still don't have a body or any evidence. Mark says I will. Meet me with a

copy of McDonnell's yearbook at Dr. Craig's office. Then I've got to swing by the house and grab my tux. Steve says you're not seriously considering going, are you? Mark says I wouldn't miss it.

ACT EIGHT

41. HOTEL

Mark runs into Jack, and nearly ruins his con. Mark presents the award, and a photo, to Bonnie. What's this? We see it's a security camera photo of Dave McDonnell at a phone booth. Mark says Dave McDonnell called from the road—says Bonnie tried to poison him and that he fears for his life. Police traced the call to this 7-Eleven, and we got the security photo. Police have an APB out for him now. Mark thinks when they catch him, he'll tell all, which should get Bonnie sent to prison for insurance fraud. She tells Mark nice try, but it will never happen. She promises to send him a postcard from the Caribbean and leaves.

42. HOTEL – NIGHT

Brilliant farce to be figured out. The long and short of it: The buy/con goes down, Killebrew shows up with the suitcase of money, and everything goes wrong. Jack's cover is blown. Killebrew runs, Jack tackles him into the pool. Eve walks by, arm-in-arm with Lloyd Largo—and looks down at Jack in the pool. You'll never change, Jack. He could learn a few things about being responsible from Lloyd.

43. MULHOLLAND – NIGHT

Bonnie drives off the road into the hills. She opens her trunk, gets out a shovel and flashlight, and dashes into the trees. She finds a spot and starts to dig . . . and that's when she's bathed in light. Mark and Steve step out, holding flashlights. Mark says I think we know who we'll find buried here. Mark guesses Dave tried to blackmail her, so she had to kill him. Since she has no taste for blood, proved by the way she killed Dr. Craig, she poisoned him and buried him up here. When Mark showed up with the photo, Bonnie had to know if Dave wasn't actually dead, if somehow he had climbed out of the shallow grave.

Bonnie says but the photo? How did you get the photo?

Mark used the yearbook photo of Dave McDonnell, scanned it into Dr. Craig's computer along with a picture he took of Steve at a phone booth. He morphed Dave's face onto Steve's.

Mark says you, of all people, ought to know better than to trust pictures. Steve says the next picture Bonnie is going to see is her own mug shot.

She hands Mark the Surgeon of the Year award—here, you deserve this.

44. HOSPITAL

Aftermath. Rita has been released and gets the entire insurance payoff. The FBI recovered all the money Killebrew stole, the art thief is in jail, and the stolen painting has been returned to Boston Museum. All's well that ends well.

THE END

About the Authors

Lee Goldberg and **William Rabkin** are veteran "showrunners" whose executive producing credits include the long-running drama *Diagnosis Murder* and the action-adventure hit *Martial Law*. Their writing and producing credits also include *seaQuest 2032, Spenser: For Hire, Hunter, Baywatch, Sliders, The Cosby Mysteries, Monk,* and *Nero Wolfe*, to name a few. Both are former journalists who have covered the television industry for *Newsweek, American Film, Electronic Media*, the *Washington Post*, the *San Francisco Chronicle*, and the *Los Angeles Times Syndicate*, among many other publications. In addition, Rabkin has directed episodes of *Diagnosis Murder* and has taught a popular television writing course at UCLA, whose graduates have written for *Roswell, Star Trek: Voyager, Farscape, Earth: Final Conflict, V.I.P.,* and *The Invisible Man*. Goldberg is also a mystery novelist (*Beyond the Beyond, My Gun Has Bullets*), and the author of a definitive book on television series development (*Unsold Television Pilots*), and he has taught writing seminars throughout the United States and as well as in as Edmonton, Canada, and Madrid, Spain.